THE BLESSED HUMAN RACE

Essays on Reconsideration

George Jochnowitz

4/22/09
To Bob,
with best
wishes,

George
川乐7c
老秀

Hamilton Books
A member of
The Rowman & Littlefield Publishing Group
Lanham · Boulder · New York · Toronto · Plymouth, UK

Copyright © 2007 by
Hamilton Books
4501 Forbes Boulevard
Suite 200
Lanham, Maryland 20706
Hamilton Books Acquisitions Department (301) 459-3366

Estover Road
Plymouth PL6 7PY
United Kingdom

Library of Congress Control Number: 2007922029
ISBN-13: 978-0-7618-3732-9 (clothbound : alk. paper)
ISBN-10: 0-7618-3732-9 (clothbound : alk. paper)
ISBN-13: 978-0-7618-3733-6 (paperback : alk. paper)
ISBN-10: 0-7618-3733-7 (paperback : alk. paper)

In memory of my parents
Helen and Jerome Jochnowitz
Who taught me to argue

Contents:

Acknowledgements

Carol, my wife, has helped me with every stage of this work, discussing my ideas with me, accompanying me on my first trip to China, and most of all, by editing the manuscript. I could have done nothing without her moral, psychological, and editorial support.

My daughter Eve was my fellow student when I began to study Chinese. She too accompanied me on my first trip to China and her enthusiasm and observations increased my understanding of what we were seeing.

My daughter Miriam accompanied me on both trips to China. We lived through the Beijing Spring experience of 1989 together. We went to Beijing together the day after the Tiananmen Massacre and to the airport the next morning. Her calmness and judgment enabled me to maintain my sanity during that frightening time. I can't imagine how I would have managed without her.

The Lewis family, who also taught at Hebei University in 1984, joined us at meals on our trips to Beijing. They made Baoding feel like home. Afterwards, Piers Lewis and I had an epistolary debate on cynicism out of which grew the last chapter of this book, which is dedicated to him.

Anne Fessenden taught at Hebei University in 1989, and her presence was a stabilizing factor during an increasingly tense period. Her interest in literature and art enriched our stay.

A conversation with my friend Franklin Horowitz inspired me to write Chapter 5.

I am grateful to all my friends for the thought-provoking conversations we have had. There are too many to list by name. I have not mentioned the names of any of my Chinese friends since discretion is the better part of valor, but I thank them all.

Parts of Chapter 2 appeared in the June 30 issue of *National Review*, copyright 1989 by National Review, 215 Lexington Avenue, New York, NY 10016. A version of Chapter 3 appeared in the No. 25 (1994) of *Outerbridge* and was reprinted in No. 28, its Retrospective Anthology issue. Versions of Chapters 4 and 5 appeared in *Partisan Review*, now defunct, in Volume 69, No. 1, (2002) and Volume 55, No. 3 (1988) respectively. Versions of Chapter 7, 9, 13, and 20 appeared in *Midstream* in January 1997, November 2001, July/August 1999, and November/December 2002 respectively. A version of Chapter 10 appeared in the Winter 1998 issue of the now defunct *Gravitas*. A version of Chapter 11 appeared in the May 1981 issue of the now defunct *Ovation*. Versions of Chapters 12, 15, 16, and 17 appeared in *And Then* Volume 3 (1990), Volume 10 (2001), Volume 5 (1993), and Volume 1 (1987) respectively. A version of Chapter 19 appeared in the now defunct Boston newspaper *Gay Community News* on October 20, 1984. I am grateful to the editors of those publications still in existence for their permission to reprint my work.

Preface

Honesty is the best policy, but it not always an easy policy to follow. The world is complicated, and truth is difficult to pin down. A half-truth can be the equivalent of a lie, as we learn from reading *Oedipus Rex* by Sophocles, a play in which Oedipus is deceived by being told part of the truth but not all.

To be honest, we have to learn, to seek, to probe, to argue. I grew up in a left-liberal home and associated questioning and debate with my parents' political views. When I lived in China, I learned that Marx had looked forward to an era when there would be no conflict because there would be no differences of opinion. This was a shattering discovery for me. I realized that the intolerance of Mao, Stalin, and Pol Pot came from the words of Marx.

One discovery led to another. If political faith leads to repression, so must religious faith. The Bible is wonderful if we explore and question it; it is dangerous if it leads us to have faith. Everything must be questioned: the greatness of Shakespeare, the meaning of familiar stories and operas, the imposition of fads and tastes upon the public, and the universal practice of telling children to finish what's on their plates. What makes humanity wonderful—and it is wonderful—is our ability to see how complex the world is and to keep exploring its vastness and its details. Our minds were programmed to make connections that they were not programmed to make. We can think thoughts that nobody ever knew were there to be thought about. Thank God.

Part I

China
Learning to reconsider

Chapter 1

Baoding Revisited

In 1984, my wife, Carol, our two college-age daughters, Eve and Miriam, and I spent the spring semester teaching at Hebei University in Baoding, an industrial city about 100 miles southwest of Beijing. On February 13, 1989, after an absence of four and a half years, my younger daughter, Miriam, and I returned to China. We arrived in Shanghai, where we would spend a few days before proceeding to Beijing, from which we would go to Baoding, where once again we would teach at Hebei University.

We immediately noticed that people's clothing was much brighter and more varied than on our previous visit in 1984. Quite a few people had curly hair. I remarked to one young man that his hair didn't look Chinese. "It's a permanent," he explained. "Is it beautiful?"

Another obvious difference was the presence of money changers. In the downtown area, you could hardly walk three feet without being approached by a man, often with blond or brown hair, saying "Change money?" I asked one where he was from, and he answered that he was a member of a Muslim minority from Xinjiang Province. There seemed to be a substantial population engaged in this profession, which is illegal but openly practiced.

Shanghai was a place in which I had only been a tourist. Beijing was different. It is only two and a half hours by train from Baoding, and we had gone there frequently. Seeing Beijing again was a great emotional experience—coming home after a long absence. I was a bit surprised at my reaction; I had never been especially fond of Beijing. But it was China the way I remembered it and understood it.

The next day we went to visit a woman we had gotten to know in New York who was a professor at Beijing University. As we approached her apartment on the campus, I was struck by how similar faculty housing at Beijing University and Hebei University were. The halls of her building were identical to ours in Baoding: the same two doors on each floor, the same bare concrete look, the same smell. Then we entered her apartment and saw the tile floor and the wallpaper. Never had we seen such a beautiful interior in China. Even more than the curly hair and money changers in Shanghai, this showed us how much China had changed.

We got to Baoding after dark, and as soon as we could, we went to see two old friends in their apartments. In both cases, there were girlie calendars on the wall, the kind that were called "cheesecake" in the 1940s. Later I saw that these calendars were found everywhere; they are the rule and not the exception. In fact, when we went to visit the city of Tianjin about a month later, we saw that the new railroad station had paintings of scantily clad women on its ceiling.

The biggest surprise of all came the next morning: the horizontal red stripe on all the buildings, walls and trees in Baoding was gone or fading. Trees now are simply unpainted. A few of the buildings are the way they used to be: white on the bottom, red stripe three feet from the ground, gray above that. Others had been repainted pink, green or yellow. I asked someone about it. "Oh that," he said. "We used to paint those stripes to show how revolutionary we were."

I found this reply quite significant; it was a statement that China no longer believed in its revolution. At the same time, it didn't seem possible; I had been in eight cities and passed through countless villages in China, but only Baoding had a red stripe. Could Baoding have held on to its revolutionary faith longer than anyplace else? I decided to ask lots of people. About half didn't know what I was talking about until I pointed to a fading stripe (there was no sense asking this question when I was indoors), and then said they had never noticed it before. Others simply said they didn't know. Still others opined that the bottom halves of buildings got dirtier faster than the top halves and had to be painted more often, and that the red stripe simply marked the level below which houses had to be painted white. Finally, a few people said that it was simply a local custom, that every town and region had its own style. This last explanation seemed the most reasonable to me.

A few months later, during our spring break in early May, we were on a train in Shanxi Province, somewhere between Taiyuan and Datong. A friend was traveling with us, a former student who is a native of Baoding. The train whizzed by a village where the houses were painted white on the bottom and gray on the top, with a red stripe separating the two colors. "Just like Baoding," we said simultaneously.

The fading of the red stripe was merely one instance of a great many changes that had taken place in Baoding. There were bright, new restaurants. There had been some drab, unpainted restaurants in 1984, with walls and floors of unpainted concrete, just like the interiors of most apartments. Now there were inviting, attractive establishments, many of which advertised Peking duck as their specialty. Dancing, which had been a daring innovation in 1984, was now a regular event. Some students were champion break dancers; indeed, one had placed second in a nation-wide contest. Faculty members were even more likely to dance than students, and there was a weekly dance in the exhibition room of the esthetics program.

If Chairman Mao had known that a Chinese university would one day teach esthetics, he might never have undertaken the Long March. Nothing was more offensive to Mao's idea of socialism than owning an object simply because it was beautiful. Except for its parks and surrounding countryside, there had been simply nothing beautiful in Baoding in 1984. The desire for beauty was considered selfishness and therefore counterrevolutionary. In 1989, on the other hand, buildings were being painted or even refaced. A new classroom building that had gone up during my absence had been designed to be attractive as well as merely utilitarian. Another building, still under construction, was decidedly modernistic. One new department store was very twentieth century in its style; another had a Ming Dynasty facade. That too reflects a contemporary mode of thinking, a desire to preserve or rediscover tradition.

Baoding had a computer store in 1989. That, if anything, represented an acceptance of the West's respect for convenience and efficiency that was so different from Mao's puritanism. On the other hand, the telephone system was still primitive. It was impossible to dial Beijing from Baoding, and waiting for a line typically took an hour. Although computers were available, cell phones had not yet come into use. And in 1989 it was still impossible to buy a round-trip ticket in China.

Americans think of China as a more formal society than the United States. In certain respects this is true; in other ways, Chinese manners are less structured and freer than American behavior.

A particular incident comes to mind. About ten days after my arrival in Baoding, I was having a hole in my bicycle tire repaired. As I was waiting for the job to be finished, a group of four students approached. I didn't recognize any of them. "In our recent discussion about you," announced one, "we said you were not interested in clothing. Is this true?"

I was delighted with their audacity. In America it is not polite to tell people you don't know very well you have been discussing them, nor is it proper to comment on another's clothing if you are not going to be complimentary. "That's right," I answered.

"Why not?"

"I'm interested in other things."

The students persisted, "What other things?"

I rejected the impulse to say sex. "Music," I replied. "How come you were discussing me?"

"We read the article you contributed to the student newspaper."

"Article? What article? Was it in English?"

"In Chinese. It was called 'Teaching at a Provincial Chinese University.'" An article of mine by that name had appeared in *The American Scholar*.

Was this a cultural difference—a difference in manners—or was it pirating? What had happened to my essay in translation? I decided not to worry but simply to feel flattered that my essay had been republished.

What is a polite question? In China, there is nothing wrong with asking, "How old are you?" or "How much money do you make?" Perhaps we Americans are too bound by formality and should be more relaxed about our ages and incomes. Other questions gave me pause: "Do all Jews have big noses like you?" "Which of your children do you prefer?"

Watching people scramble to board a bus in Baoding makes New York seem the paragon of decorum. Service in the local post office is faster and more courteous than in New York, but in Baoding there is no such thing as forming a line when buying stamps. As for traffic, it just moves; nobody looks, nobody stops. What will happen when there are more cars?

Chinese culture demands the scrupulous repayment of favors. There were a few students from Baoding studying in America whom I had been able to help. Their relatives in China overwhelmed my daughter and me with hospitality. They rented or borrowed vans to drive us around, cooked elaborate meals for us, and treated us to banquets in hotel dining rooms. A banquet is indeed a formal occasion, with course after course and innumerable toasts. Still, how formal can you be when using chopsticks to eat fish with bones? It is Americans and not Chinese who worry about table manners. Nevertheless, my hosts may have found me rude; I never downed the contents of my glass after each *ganbei* ("bottoms up," literally "dry glass"). I have never understood why anyone should ever want to get drunk. One characteristic China shares with America is the presence of heavy drinkers.

When Americans bump into passersby, they say "Excuse me," but Chinese rarely say *duibuqi* under similar circumstances. When you ask for something in a Chinese department store, the answer is usually *meiyou* (there isn't any), although the item may be in plain view. On the other hand, people went to enormous lengths to be helpful to me on occasion. When my printer didn't work, a man I had never seen before spent three hours helping me. I never learned his name, so I can never repay his favor.

Good manners should serve the purpose of making human interactions smoother, easier and more pleasant. Sometimes formality is the best way to achieve this, sometimes not. Manners should break barriers rather than build them. To get back to the four students who wanted to know about my interest in clothing, I think they did the right thing. Americans are very good at waiting in line, which certainly makes life more agreeable. But I think the Chinese are better at making friends quickly.

My students were English majors, and a certain percentage of them were destined to become teachers. Chinese students did not choose their own jobs in 1989; the university assigned them to the positions they would theoretically hold for life. There is a great deal of dissatisfaction with this system, and things had gotten a bit freer than they were in 1984, but job assignment was still a source of anxiety, especially for the seniors. There were two things the students particularly feared: being sent to a place they didn't want to go, which occasionally meant separation from a fiancé or fiancée, and being assigned a job as a teacher. Teachers are not respected and do not get paid a decent wage, I was told again and again.

Here are unedited excerpts from compositions handed in to me by two of my own students. In the first, the author claims to be quoting a ten-year-old elementary-school dropout.

> Nowadays, the most important thing for us is to earn money, money
> is most powerful in our society. I can earn a lot of money everyday,

much more than a University Professor do. Why should I go to school? It's not worthwhile to be educated!

Everybody knows clearly that China's education is in a very bad situation. Teachers' lower wages, lack of lodgings, humble social status and meagre investment of the government throw the Chinese intellectual into despair

On April 11th, I was asked to give a public lecture about college education in the United States. Afterwards, I was interviewed by reporters from the local radio station. There was a question that both my audience at the lecture and the reporters in my apartment asked me: "Why are Chinese students disillusioned with education?" I said that in the final stage of communism, according to Marx, there would be no specialization, no trade and no distinctions between country and city. A nation that believed in such a philosophy would at best be grudgingly tolerant toward education, and at worst, do what China had done during the Cultural Revolution and make being educated a punishable offense. No one took issue with what I said. Chinese people, it seemed to me, had both the desire and the freedom (or should I say the courage?) to complain.

Hebei University is located at the eastern edge of Baoding. East of the campus there are farms where cabbages, tomatoes and melons are raised. A bit down the road are large, flat wheat fields—the wheat is green, tall and heavy in April and May. At least, that's the way it was in 1989. But even then, one could see that the city was spreading.

The western half of Baoding is heavily industrial, and we rarely went there. One day during our earlier stay in 1984, however, Kathy Lewis (a member of the other American family teaching there at that time), my wife and I decided to walk around western Baoding simply because it was there. Inside a walled compound with several factory buildings, we saw what looked like a Protestant church. This aroused our curiosity, so we entered the compound and took a picture of the building. Before we could leave the compound, three young men stopped us and told us to sit down in an office. Of the three of us, I was the best Chinese speaker, although this was not saying too much. They asked who we were and why we had come. I answered we had simply been strolling and were curious about the church building. They took my film and tried to tell me what kind of place we had entered, but my Chinese was not good enough to understand their explanation. Then they asked what country we were from. We said "America," which must have been the right answer. They said we could go, told us not to come back, and added one word in English: "Sorry."

For five years I wondered what kind of place I had stumbled into. One of the reasons I wanted to go back to Baoding in 1989 was to learn the answer to this question. I told the story to one of my students and asked him to accompany me to the church. He had never heard of such a place and was quite amazed at the complicated route I took him through, to a neighborhood he had never seen. We found the place and asked to see the manager. He was quite apologetic, but said he hadn't been there in 1984 and had no idea where to find my film. He was sure it would no longer be good anyway. He explained that 1984 was not all that long after the Cultural Revolution, and people were still very nervous about letting foreigners take pictures. As for the building, it had never been a church but had once been a Protestant school, and that certainly I could take a photograph of it. All I had to do was fill out an application and submit it to the police, who would be sure to give their consent.

Nothing has changed, I thought. "Application?" I said. "I don't want to bother. I'm just curious. What is this place?"

"An underwear factory," he answered. The mystery of why my film was taken is still unsolved. I guess underwear is supposed to be hidden.

Chapter 2

Beijing Spring

My second stay in China can be divided into two distinct periods: before April 22nd—the date of the memorial service for Party Secretary Hu Yaobang—and after. The second half was dominated by the fact that China was going through an extraordinary period in its history and perhaps in the history of the world. The people were rising up against a totalitarian state.

April 22 was the day demonstrations began in Beijing, the day of the funeral of former Secretary Hu Yaobang. That was also the day political protest posters called *da zi bao* (big character posters) began to go up on campus. A surprising number of students got on the train to Beijing that day, feeling there was no way they could express their sentiments in quiet old Baoding. But on Monday, April 24th, there was a demonstration even in Baoding, the first of many. Students left Hebei University and headed for the campus of North China Electric Power Institute, a few blocks away, but the students there had been locked into the campus and could not leave to join the demonstration. After the students had walked to the Baoding Communist Party headquarters and back to the campus, they heard the university loudspeakers exhorting them to stick to their studies and stay out of trouble.

Except for the week of Spring Holiday, when almost everyone left the campus, demonstrations continued from April 24th until the Tiananmen Massacre on June 4th. Sometimes they were planned; other times they were spontaneous. Sometimes they were done in conjunction with North China Electric Power Institute and Hebei Agricultural University; sometimes workers from local factories joined; sometimes the demonstration was restricted to Hebei University. Some were during the day; others, at night. On many occasions the students tossed bottles from their dormitory windows, a practice I did not understand until someone pointed out to me the fact that the *Xiaoping* in Deng Xiaoping's name sounds exactly the same as *xiao ping*, meaning "little bottle."

In Baoding, most of the city went about its business, only occasionally stopping to look at or join with the students. But there were times when Hebei University was as filled with the spirit of the Democracy Movement as Tiananmen Square itself. There was the time a group of workers marched into the campus at night. They were greeted with rousing cheers by the students, literally rousing, getting out of bed to join on a midnight march through the city. There were the times students marched to Hebei University from one of the other universities or two-year colleges in town. There were the times one heard shouts of *"Da dao Li Peng"* (Down with Li Peng) from the windows of the boys' dorm. In addition to tossing little bottles, *xiao ping*, from their windows, they also threw flaming newspapers from the windows, a practice I considered quite dangerous, since the papers floated slowly down to the ground, drifting this way and that as they fell, not all that unlikely to float into an open window on a lower floor.

Nor was Baoding unique in this respect. Demonstrations took place not only in big cities but in medium-sized ones, not only in Shanghai and Canton but in Taiyuan and Shijiazhuang, in Baodings all over China. When we visited Inner Mongolia University in Hohhot on May 4th, during our spring break, we could see that posters had been torn off the bulletin boards. A banner stretched across the front of the building facing the entrance to the campus exhorted students to love their country and study hard.

When I woke up on the morning of Tuesday, May 16th, my daughter was not home. I assumed she was out jogging, but I learned at breakfast that she had gone with a demonstration which had left the campus at 6 A.M. She returned at ten and said that the students had been asking for me. I hopped on my bicycle and headed to the Party Headquarters, where I saw about a thousand people sitting in front of the entrance. A group of people surrounded me and began asking me questions in Chinese. I answered as well as I could, given my poor knowledge of the Chinese language. I said I thought the students were the hope of China and predicted that in a year China would be a free country. It was quite hot in the sun, and I saw an ice cream vendor not far away. I stepped away from the crowd, but before I could buy my ice cream, a man in his twenties grabbed my arm and started pulling me away. "Who are you?" I asked in my best Chinese. It sounded to me as if he said he was a *xiansheng*, which could mean "husband," "master" or "teacher." I didn't know whether he wanted to say he was a gentleman, an ordinary citizen, or the boss. "What does *xiansheng* mean?" I inquired in Chinese. "I don't speak any foreign language," he replied, shoving me into the department store and telling me to go back to my campus. I assume he was an undercover cop.

That evening, almost everyone I met told me they had seen me on the local television news program. The next day, two policemen came to the campus to visit me. My daughter Miriam joined me, and we heard the officers tell me I had broken the law, and that I would be responsible for any consequences if I did so again. Miriam asked if it was illegal to demonstrate in China (I have been told that the Chinese constitution says protest is allowed) and was told it was illegal for foreigners to interfere in Chinese internal affairs. My daughter asked for a definite answer to her question: Are demonstrations legal or not? Yes or no? The man acting as our interpreter tried to conceal his delight. The policemen refused to answer.

Beijing was special. The spirit of the moment pervaded the whole city. For a very brief period in May, while President Mikhail Gorbachev of the USSR was in Beijing, China actually had a free press. Reporters joined the demonstrators, holding their own marches. The 7 o'clock evening news showed what was happening in Tiananmen. That was when I got hooked on the news. I gave up my regular evening walk through the farms east of Hebei University and watched television. After martial law was declared, unfortunately, television news, like everything else, became profoundly depressing.

There has never been a public opinion poll in China; it would be unthinkable, since it would suggest that the people knew what they wanted better than the Party did. No one knows what China's 800 million peasants think. I can tell you about two of them, not a very big sample. One was an old man I spoke to, through an interpreter, in the village of Dazhai, on April 29th. "In agriculture, learn from Dazhai," said Chairman Mao, and for years Dazhai was a tourist attraction. Today few people go there, but the villagers are relatively sophisticated; they did not run up to form circles around us and stare, as happens so frequently when foreigners stray off the beaten path.

"You have lived through a lot of history," I said to the old man. "How have things changed through your life?"

"They've always been the same," he said, to my great surprise. Did he mean that there was no difference before and after Liberation?

"Our work is always the same," he repeated through my translator, my former student Wu Shujia (all students' names in this book are pseudonyms), who was traveling with us.

"What do you think of the student demonstrations?"

He had never heard of them. They had only just begun. I told him about them, but he showed no interest.

The second peasant was a woman. On May 18th, when the students at Hebei University took over the loudspeakers and appealed for money to establish an independent newspaper, she heard the appeal, walked over to the campus and dropped 50 *yuan* into the collection box. That was about two weeks' salary for the average Chinese worker in 1989.

Sidewalk peddlers sometimes signaled me to come over and talk to them. Like the students, they were hungry to learn about the world. "What do you think of the students?" was usually the first question.

"China's hope," was my prepared answer. This invariably elicited a smile and a thumbs up sign. Sometimes I was asked a second question: "What do you think of the Communist Party?"

"It serves no purpose."

Thumbs up. "And what do you think of Marxism?"

"Gou pi" ("bullshit," literally "dog fart"), I would say. This got the biggest smile of all, but did not always elicit a thumbs up. If I said it to a student, I generally would get an argument: "You haven't read all of Marx. Marxism has never been attempted anywhere."

My sample was not only small but self-selected and therefore quite unreliable, since I only talked politics to those peddlers who spoke to me first.

Nevertheless, it led me to the tentative conclusion that peddlers are more anti-Marxist than students, which is not altogether surprising, since they are practicing capitalists.

There seemed to be no one in Beijing at all who supported the government, although I did meet some who did during our spring-break trip, especially in Shanxi Province. They were typically Party members in their sixties. They considered demonstrations disorderly by definition, said they did not like discussing politics, and said it would be a tragedy if socialism were abandoned because then all the suffering that had taken place since Liberation would have been for naught.

China has never had an election. No one can say what the will of the people is. Nor can anyone know how many Chinese really understand what democracy means. Perhaps the great majority are uninterested in what went on in Tiananmen Square. Perhaps most of China still loves Chairman Mao. Perhaps. But I doubt it. The movement was national. In Beijing it was unanimous. It grew despite China's lack of telephones and censored press. It grew despite the danger of violence and imprisonment that was always present, that everybody knew about, and that a substantial portion of the population had experienced personally.

The French Revolution, the American Revolution, Liberation itself—all succeeded despite open divisions among the French, American and Chinese people of the time. On the other hand, there was no visible popular opposition to the Chinese Democracy Movement. So how did the government succeed in suppressing it?

Part of the answer lies in the fact that China is simultaneously the most political and least political of countries. It is the most political in that ubiquitous billboards bear political slogans, children wear red scarves to indicate their membership in the Young Pioneers, and English majors writing their senior theses before graduation describe whatever novel they happen to write about as proof of the cruelty and hypocrisy of capitalist society. It is the least political in that there is no independent political organization of any kind. There is no way to try to get local authorities to fix a hole in the pavement or change a bus route.

I fought a battle with the local post office. There always was a metal track from their accordion-style door stretched over the ground at the entrance. When I almost broke my neck over it the first time I entered, I told them *"hen weixian"* (very dangerous). *"Mingtian xiuli,"* they said (they would fix it the next day). The next day, when I tripped on it again, I told them *"hen weixian."* They fixed it right then and there, but the day after that it was back. *"Hen weixian,"* I said. Nobody did or said anything. I went with a translator and told them an old person might get hurt. *"Mingtian xiuli,"* they said. I persisted. It took four months, but they finally removed the hazard. After I left Baoding, I was informed by a friend that the obstacle had come back. Who knows if any old people have broken limbs over it.

What I was doing was acting politically. I was temporarily successful because I was a foreigner. Chinese people are not supposed to engage in independent political action. There is no way for public issues, major or minor, to be addressed. No citizen would ever suggest that it is the duty of the post office to keep the entranceway safe and free from obstruction. A Chinese who wanted to report a hazard at a post office entrance would have had to make the issue a personal one, and would have tried to persuade an individual employee to deal with the danger as a voluntary private act. In a country where civil society existed, a group of local residents could have organized to get the post office to correct the problem.

Once I visited the parents of a student from China who was studying at the College of Staten Island in 1989. When Hebei University had its spring vacation, my daughter Miriam and I went to the home town of my student. I got to his parents' apartment house and found that there was some water coming from a neighboring construction site which trickled by the entrance of the building. Algae was growing there, making it very hard to get into the building without slipping. I was told to hold on to the wall so I wouldn't fall. My friend's mother had fallen a few weeks earlier and was still in the hospital. We visited her the following day and commented on how dangerous the entrance to her building was. "I was careless," she said. If the accident had happened today, she might not have blamed herself but would have sued.

Lawsuits are not nice things, but the fact that they now are possible makes China a better place—a freer place—than it was before.

Once, to my amazement, I was told that there were independent political parties in China and introduced to a leader of such a party some time before the Democracy Movement started. I very much wanted to meet him and find out what his party stood for and what it did. Although I met him and spoke to him, I never found out what his party's positions were and how it operated. What I learned was that this party considered itself subordinate to the Party. Could being subordinate have been its only purpose?

In a country with no politics there is no way for ordinary people to make their views known and no avenue for change from the bottom. There is no possible connection between talking about politics and doing something about it. All innovations come from the top and are transmitted and enforced through the hierarchical structure of the Party. New directives coming from the Party leaders can change life quite abruptly, which makes Chinese society extremely unstable.

And then politics happened. If I hadn't seen it I wouldn't have believed it. The popularity of the Democracy Movement was overwhelming. On Friday, May 19th, Miriam and I went to Beijing for the weekend in order to buy airplane tickets. Even before our train arrived, we could perceive the spirit of the place. Houses facing the railroad tracks were covered with big-character posters: "We love students." In Beijing posters were on the walls, on subways, everywhere: "The people love students," "Workers love students," even "Communist Party members love students"! Ambulances were going back and forth, carrying unconscious hunger strikers to the hospital. The demonstrators had assumed the almost impossible job of directing traffic, in order to keep lanes open for the ambulances, and were succeeding beyond anyone's wildest expectations.

We went to Tiananmen Square to see if we could recognize anyone from Hebei University. It was like looking for a needle in a haystack, except that we found the needle. First we saw a banner with Chinese characters saying "Baoding," then another saying "Hebei University." Our students recognized us, applauded, shook our hands, offered us soft drinks and gave us headbands announcing our support for the hunger strikers. We didn't know that at the same moment, other students of ours were blocking the 27th Army as it was passing through Baoding on its way to Beijing. They detained it for several hours. We certainly could never have guessed that it would be the 27th Army that would be blamed for all the gratuitous violence of June 4th.

The crowds in Tiananmen were composed almost exclusively of the young, to be sure, but the whole city was feeding them and visiting them. Railroad employees, whom I generally found rude and uncooperative, were allowing anyone with student ID to ride free to Beijing. As for the demonstrators, they may have been defying the government, but they certainly were not thumbing their noses at society. Indeed, they made a point of their patriotism and repeatedly sang both the Chinese National Anthem and the Internationale.

We were staying at the Friendship Hotel, miles from the center of Beijing. It was soon clear that that was a mistake; on our way from Tiananmen Square back to the hotel, the subway train stopped at a station and there was an announcement that all service was suspended until further notice. We got into the street and stopped a man on a tricycle cart. We asked what he would charge us to go to the Friendship Hotel. He looked at the headbands our students had given us. "You were in the Square? You can ride free," he said. We paid him anyway.

The next morning we learned there was no bus, subway or taxi service in the city. But we spent the day with old Chinese friends, visiting Beijing University and then going out for Peking duck. One of our friends was a neighbor of the dissident astrophysicist Fang Lizhi and took us to Professor Fang's apartment, where we chatted briefly about politics. After our chat, as we walked through the streets wearing the headbands our students had given us, passersby applauded and made the "V" for "Victory" sign. All ten million of Beijing's citizens were rejoicing; I had never seen so much happiness. Trucks carrying food and beverages to Tiananmen Square kept passing by. Feeding the million demonstrators in Beijing was a task that required organization and a great deal of effort. A city-wide drop in crime, accidents and fires was reported.

On the walk back to the Friendship Hotel after leaving our friends, we passed a banner stretched across the road: "The People's Army protects the people." How very different the Chinese students were from the American counter-culture protesters who said, "Off the pigs." The optimistic mood of the young people was reminiscent of the 1960's; several observers have compared Beijing to Woodstock. However, I believe the differences were greater than the similarities. The students in Beijing were in danger and they knew it. The hunger strikers were obviously risking their lives, but so was everyone else in the Square. Demonstrators wrote their wills before going to Tiananmen; events proved they were not just making a dramatic gesture. Even though the mood of the demonstrators was cheerful, no one looked upon the event as fun. The constant wail of the sirens of ambulances carrying off unconscious hunger strikers was enough to prove that this was not a game.

When we got back to the Friendship Hotel, Ai Heshui, one the friends I had spent the day with, said he would be bicycling downtown where he would spend the night. He gave me various documents he was carrying, saying he was afraid of losing them. I was afraid he might not succeed in getting back to the hotel Sunday morning since there already was no public transportation and the traffic situation might get worse, but he answered that if that happened, I should take his papers to Baoding with me and he would pick them up in my apartment. I didn't put two and two together. That night, at exactly the point where I saw the banner saying that the army loved the people, a crowd of students and local people blocked the street and persuaded the army to turn back. From my hotel window, I could hear chanting, then what sounded like shots and finally a great deal of traffic. Miriam slept through the whole thing. I didn't know who had won until Ai Heshui called at 6 A.M. and said he was one of the many people who had faced the army down. He came to our room to reclaim his documents.

People I have spoken to and written to say that the first attempt of the People's Liberation Army to enter Beijing took place in the early morning hours of Saturday, May 20, but we walked around the Haidian neighborhood all day Saturday, and there was no indication that anything had happened. But it was Sunday, May 21st, not Saturday, May 20th, when Ai Heshui called us and came to our room. My own experience contradicts the reports of when the Army tried to enter the city but was turned back.

That morning, Sunday May 21st, we managed to get to the railroad station with the help of a delivery man with a tricycle cart, a *san lun che*. Martial law had been declared, and foreigners had disappeared from the streets. We were relieved to take a train back to Baoding, where we still felt safe.

Chapter 3

We Flee China

"I made a special trip to Baoding just to warn you," said Gao Xuesheng, who had been my student the previous time I had taught at Hebei University, in 1984. "Get out of the country. Leave China as soon as possible. Something terrible is going to happen."

"What sort of terrible thing?" I asked, feeling he must be right.

"Please don't ask me. Please don't ask me how I know. I came here because I'm your friend."

If Gao Xuesheng had been a native speaker of English his words would have sounded overly dramatic and perhaps unconvincing. In this case, speaking what was for him a foreign language made him more eloquent, and he was very persuasive indeed. "I have tickets for June 11th, just two weeks from now," I said. "Miriam and I will fly to Tokyo on the 11th and go from there to New York."

"Leave sooner if you can. Lots of people know what you've been saying and doing. When the police came to warn you and Miriam not to go on any more demonstrations, you said, 'The worst they can do is deport me.'"

"Did I tell you that?" I inquired, thinking my statement had been harmless enough.

"No you didn't. Don't ask me how I know. Get out while you can. Something awful will happen. I know what I'm talking about."

Gao Xuesheng was saying what I had been thinking: June 11th wasn't soon enough. My daughter Miriam and I had grown increasingly unhappy after the declaration of martial law on May 20th. Our hopes for the democracy movement had vanished. Our students were boycotting classes, so there was not much for us to do at Hebei University. Gao Xuesheng's words were alarming, but I was nervous anyway. Now I had an excuse to do something besides fret, and enough motivation to go through the effort of making a phone call.

Calling Beijing from Baoding, a mere hundred miles away, was much harder than it should have been. China doesn't have enough telephone lines. There was no direct dialing from Baoding. Making a call involved going downstairs to the Foreign Affairs Office (which, despite its name, was only in charge of paying us "foreign experts" our salaries and attending to our needs) and asking Mr. Zhu to place a call. Mr. Zhu spoke no English, but my Chinese was good enough to give him the number and name of the person I wanted to call. Then I would fidget in the office, or at least within the building, until a line became available and the call could go through. This usually took about an hour.

I called our travel agent the next morning. She said it was too late to cancel my cut-rate reservation. I told her to leave my Tokyo-to-New York flight unchanged, but to get Miriam and me on the earliest available plane from Beijing to Tokyo whatever the cost. She was able to reserve seats on a June 6th flight and told me to pick up the tickets in her Beijing office on Friday the second. Gao Xuesheng volunteered to accompany me to Beijing. I picked up the tickets. Then I went for my last look at Tiananmen Square.

The portable toilets on the east side of the square stank. The demonstrators, dirty and exhausted, had been both rained on and baked by the sun; they looked weak and helpless. I remembered how extraordinarily attractive the million demonstrators in Beijing had looked two or three weeks earlier. The government would certainly consider the statue of the Goddess of Democracy a provocation.

"They're dead," I thought. "Why don't they escape while they still can?"

Saturday, back in Baoding, I ran across Nian Qingshi (not his real name), a young teacher I hardly knew. We chatted, and I expressed surprise that a movement as overwhelmingly popular as the Democracy Movement had been could weaken so quickly.

"Don't you fear death?" he asked rhetorically.

"I'm leaving China Tuesday," I replied, implicitly answering his question in the affirmative.

"There's a report about you and Miriam. You've been to demonstrations in Baoding and Beijing, and you've visited Fang Lizhi. The report says your behavior contrasts most unfavorably with that of the Japanese foreign experts."

It was no longer surprising to me that everyone knew everything about us. Being a foreign expert in Baoding meant being a local celebrity. I knew enough about China to realize that going to see a demonstration or visiting a dissident would be considered provocative. I thanked Nian Qingshi for the information. Although the news gave me something further to worry about, I realized his telling me was a gesture of solidarity. He had learned something he wasn't supposed to know, and the wishes of those in authority were being subverted by revealing their secrets about me.

Nian Qingshi and Gao Xuesheng both seemed to know that Miriam and I were considered troublemakers. The thought entered my head that we wouldn't be allowed to leave China, but I decided that was extremely unlikely. I had no trouble falling asleep that night. An hour or two later, however, I was awakened by the sound of shouting under our windows. I had often heard the sounds of midnight demonstrations during the preceding six weeks, but this was very loud and didn't go away. Miriam went downstairs and learned that all the pro-democracy big-character posters on campus had just been torn down.

These hand-written posters, which had been put up by the more politically active students starting in late April, had changed the nature of life at Hebei

University. Crowds gathered in front of the bulletin boards and walls and copied down the posters' messages in their notebooks. But now, Mr. Han, the Communist Party Secretary of Hebei University, had given the order to remove them, and so the students were demonstrating under his windows, which happened to be adjacent to our windows, since the foreign experts and the university administrators lived in the same building—the best on campus.

The noise prevented me from sleeping, but I was happy. The students were wonderful—China's hope. I did not know, the students did not know—perhaps even Mr. Han did not know—that at that moment hundreds and perhaps thousands of unarmed citizens were being killed by the People's Liberation Army (PLA) on the streets leading into Tiananmen Square. In retrospect, I surmise that Mr. Han was unaware that he was carrying out an order deliberately timed to coincide with the PLA invasion of Beijing.

When dawn came, I decided to stroll around campus before breakfast. There was no reason for anyone to be awake so early, but I noticed a young woman walking around carrying a portable radio. 6:30 A.M. was usually when the Voice of America's English-language programs came in clearest, and so I assumed she was listening to VOA. The whole campus had been hooked on VOA for weeks. I walked over to hear what the latest headlines were. That was how I learned about the Tiananmen massacre.

The fact that Gao Xuesheng had told me something terrible would happen, the fact that I had looked at the demonstrators in the square two days earlier and thought them doomed, did not lessen the shock. As I entered my building, a call was coming through from Carol, my wife, in New York. She thought Miriam and I might have been in Beijing over the weekend, as we so frequently were. I assured her we were safe in Baoding where there had been no violence.

It was Sunday morning, but the Foreign Affairs Office was open, no doubt because Miriam and I were scheduled to leave Baoding the following day. Preparations had been made to give Miriam and me a farewell banquet in the evening, to accompany us to Beijing on Monday and help us with our luggage, and to help us get back the 2,500 yuan ($700) deposit that we had been forced to leave on my laptop computer when we landed in Shanghai in February. Apparently the customs official was afraid I would sell it and not pay duty.

The director of the Foreign Affairs Office was called Black Guo, which distinguishes him from Tall Guo, who, like Black Guo, was a member of the faculty of the Foreign Language Department. Black Guo got his nickname in junior high school, when he played a role in a minstrel show. After making a few phone calls, Black Guo learned that there was no rail service to Beijing, and that the roads were closed to all but military traffic. While we sat in his office wondering what to do next, a call came through from a young faculty member who had eyewitnessed the massacre a few blocks west of Tiananmen Square. After hearing the awful things our colleague had seen, Black Guo asked him whether one could drive through the streets of Beijing.

"*Zoubuliao*" (can't get through) said Black Guo upon hanging up, repeating what had been told to him over the phone. It was a phrase I would hear many times in the next few days. I decided to call the American Embassy to ask for their advice. The official I spoke to was sure that one of the university chauffeurs would know the local roads and could get us to the airport by going around Beijing. I thanked him and hung up before I realized that he hadn't asked for my name and phone number. It would have been nice for the Embassy to know we existed, but calling back was just too time-consuming.

Black Guo said he would get us a police permit to enable us to cross the army barricades on the roads to Beijing and speak to the university garage about getting us a car and a driver. I went upstairs to give Miriam the latest news, but she told me her news first: "*Meiyou dianle, meiyou shuile,*" (The electricity and water have gone off). Miriam and I ordinarily spoke to each other in English, of course, but the news that there was no water or electricity was something we had been told in Chinese much more frequently than we had ever heard it in English. The words just came more spontaneously in Chinese. It was normal for there not to be electricity on Sunday, but we usually were warned a day or so before the water went off so we could stock up.

Under normal circumstances, we would have been annoyed not to have water to flush the toilet, but we were grieving for China and wondering how—and if—we would get to the airport. We decided to continue packing. Black Guo invited us to lunch at his house. He had been unable to persuade a chauffeur to drive us to the airport. He and the president of the university spent the next few hours on the phone nagging a driver to take us.

"Here we are in a totalitarian country, and they can't even find us a driver," said Miriam.

There was nothing to do but wait. At four there was a knock at the door. It was my student Huo Tou. Whoever said that all Chinese students are diligent? Huo Tou came late to class, if he came at all. He was late again; he had said he would come at 2:30. He waved a bottle of wine in the air and said, "I have good news. Ayatollah Khomeini is dead. Who knows? Maybe one day Deng Xiaoping can also die. There is hope for China."

"The Baoding psychic has predicted that Deng Xiaoping will die on September 14th," I told him. The psychic was a 20-year-old man who had never been wrong, according to local report.

"Let's drink a toast to the death of aged tyrants," said Huo Tou with great emotion. We clinked glasses. "*Ganbei*" (bottoms up). "Did you hear a demonstration leaving campus about two hours ago?" continued Huo Tou. "Did you hear what they were chanting? *Da dao Gongchandang!*" (Down with the Communist Party).

"Really? I can't believe it!"

"Really," said Huo Tou in a mixture of delight and rage. "Yesterday no one would have said it or even wanted to say it. The Party has lost everyone's respect. It's about time."

At 6:30, Miriam and I went to our farewell banquet. It could not have been more inappropriate. The food was delicious, but no one was hungry. President Yu gave us our going-away presents. She told us the driver would pick us up at 9 o'clock the next morning. Black Guo would have our police pass, and we would be accompanied by Mr. Zhu of the Foreign Affairs Office and Zhang Qiping, a graduate student who would be our translator if we needed one.

That night, Miriam and I went out for a yogurt. We saw a huge crowd in front of the library. People had just gathered to talk and cry. Lots of students were away, and nobody knew who had gone to Tiananmen and who had simply gone home. The atmosphere was like a house of mourning.

Monday at nine the chauffeur was nowhere to be found. We waited in front of our building together with the friends who had come to see us off. "Remember the psychic—September 14th," said one friend. "Kill them. Hang them," muttered another under her breath. Finally at eleven, the car and driver showed up. Mr. Zhu, Zhang Qiping, Miriam and I got into the car. As we drove off, a voice called after us, "When you come back to Baoding, China will be free!" I couldn't hold back the tears.

There was almost no traffic on the Beijing Highway. It normally took four hours to go by car from Baoding to Beijing, almost twice as long as by train, because one was always getting caught behind a cart drawn by a draft animal. But on June 5th, the donkeys and mules were having a day off. The wheat fields had begun to turn from green to yellow; harvest time was approaching. We stopped for lunch at an Islamic restaurant along the road and then proceeded smoothly until we reached the army road block. Mr. Zhu stepped out and showed the soldiers our police permit.

They were not interested. "Permit or no permit, nobody can go through here."

"*Zoubuliao*," said the driver. "Let's go back to Baoding."

Mr. Zhu is a Party member and a good Communist. So were the soldiers, no doubt. They had been studying Marx all their lives and knew there was no motivation except for money. "They've already paid for their airplane reservations," said Mr. Zhu.

That was an irrefutable argument. The soldiers looked at our tickets and then waved us through.

Soon we reached a toll bridge. "And where might you be going?" asked the toll collector.

"Beijing," we answered.

"Ha, ha. They're going to Beijing," said the toll collector.

The driver didn't say *zoubuliao*, but his facial expression indicated he was thinking it.

We entered Beijing from the south. The airport is northeast of the city, and we turned right (east) at San Huan Lu (Third Ring Road), trying to avoid downtown. The road turned north in its circular path through the city. Before long, we saw a few burnt army trucks—the paint was blistered, discolored, or gone; the metal misshapen by the heat of the fire; the upholstery and tires just ashes. Then we saw a whole row of them, in a straight line. Many were still smoldering. After a while, Miriam began to count them. She counted over thirty; we estimate there were about twenty before she started to count. What had happened to the soldiers? Why were the vehicles in a row? Had there been bloodshed? How can unarmed civilians burn fifty army trucks?

There apparently had been some kind of major battle in southeastern Beijing. We were not on any direct route to Tiananmen Square. The fact that some trucks were still smoldering suggested they had been set on fire after the massacre. Had the soldiers just abandoned their trucks and run away? I have no answers.

We continued north until we saw that the street was blocked by busses, some of them burnt and without tires, standing perpendicular across the road. We made a U-turn and tried another street. More buses. We stopped a passerby, who said that the local residents had blocked the streets to prevent the army from moving through the city. "How do we get to the airport?" we asked. "*Zoubuliao*, he answered.

We were near Jianguomen, a part of the city I knew. A few days later the bridge over the highway at Jianguomen would be the site of a ceremony in memory of a soldier who had been killed there by angry citizens. We were not far from the American Embassy and decided to go there to see if they could be of help. A lot of activity was going on; a convoy was about to leave in order to evacuate Americans from the Haidian area, where Beijing University and most of the city's other institutions of higher learning are located. One consular official told us the Embassy was understaffed and underequipped; Haidian was a potential trouble spot and Americans there had to be gotten out quickly; we had our own transportation and could get to the airport by ourselves. Another official gave us a map and some general instructions on how to leave.

Our driver got out of the car and sat on the sidewalk. "*Zoubuliao*," he said. The only place he would go was back to Baoding.

At that moment a car pulled up and several people got out. The man who had given us the map told us to speak to an American woman who had stepped out of the car. She had just come from the airport. She approached us and said, "*Meiyou wenti*" (No problem). She drew a zigzag line on our map and told us if we followed it, we would avoid all roadblocks. She went to our driver, sitting sullenly on the sidewalk, and said "*meiyou wenti*." She told him many times in Chinese that if we followed the route she had drawn, we would make it.

He tried hard not to groan and got back into the car. We made it to the vicinity of the airport without a *wenti*, although we passed lots of soldiers along the way. The next problem was getting a hotel room for the night. At the second hotel we went to, the manager said there was one room with two single beds.

"Tell the manager three of us can sleep on the floor," I said.

"It's against regulations," translated our interpreter, Zhang Qiping.

"Tell him this is a dangerous time. New roadblocks may be set up. If we spend the night in separate hotels, we may not be able to rejoin."

"What if an inspector comes?"

It seemed highly unlikely to me that hotel inspectors would be making their rounds in a city at war, but I felt this argument would cut no ice with the manager. "Tell him we'll pay for an extra room even if we all sleep in the same room," I tried.

Zhang Qiping and the manager had begun to raise their voices. The manager walked away; he certainly wouldn't help us if he got angry. Although his disagreement had been with me, he had been shouting at Zhang Qiping, not at me; he and I could still be civil. I wasn't sure my Chinese would be good enough, but I tried. "I know you want to help us," I began; "you've given my daughter and me a room. But if we're separated from our friends, we won't be able to get to the airport."

"*Meiyou*" (there isn't any), said the manager.

"*Zemma ban?*" (What's to be done?) I asked. Experience had taught me that was the best answer to *meiyou*.

The manager relented. "Come back in an hour. I'll see what I can arrange." Success! When I returned, he had found two vacant rooms.

The airport the next morning was filled with many very nervous people, as was to be expected. Miriam waited on one line to check our eight suitcases; I waited on another to pay the airport exit tax, only it wasn't a line—it was a crowd of tense people shoving. After an hour, I was no closer to the window. Our plane was scheduled to leave in ten minutes. One man seemed to be an experienced shover; he was going to get to the window first. "Buy two for me, please," I requested, giving him the right amount of money. "And three for me," said the woman in back of me. The man got five extra airport tax receipts for us, enabling us to catch our plane and subtracting three people from the shoving crowd instead of one.

Miriam had reached the head of the check-in line, which looked much more like a line. Then Zhang Qiping appeared. While we were dealing with our lines, he had gotten our 2,500 yuan deposit back. I had given up hope of seeing the money again. I still wasn't sure what we could do with it. The plane was about to leave, and Chinese money could be exchanged only in China (this was foreign exchange certificates; the other kind of Chinese money, *renminbi*, could not be exchanged at all).

"Don't worry," said Zhang Qiping. "There was just an announcement that your plane's departure has been delayed by half an hour."

We thanked Zhang Qiping and Mr. Zhu and embraced them. They had voluntarily risked the dangers of traveling through Beijing in order to help us leave China. We told them to thank the driver, who had gone to the parking lot and was waiting in the car. He had feared for his life, which was not unreasonable, and he—like Zhang Qiping and Mr. Zhu—was still facing a trip back to Baoding. We are indeed grateful for what these three men did for us.

We changed our 2,500 yuan into Japanese yen. It was late, but we were not the last people to board the plane; a Japanese family of three rushed on after us. "We're in the twentieth century," said Miriam with relief. She had hit the nail on the head. What's wrong with China's political system—what makes totalitarianism so frightening—is its rejection of free thought and therefore of science and modernity.

When we reached Carol on the phone to tell her we were safe in Japan, at 6 A.M. New York time, she answered at the first ring. It was clear she had been much more frightened than Miriam and I. We called Baoding the next day and were extremely relieved to learn that our driver, Zhang Qiping and Mr. Zhu had returned safely. We had not planned to spend five days in Tokyo; it was the result of moving up the date of our flight from China. We were not in the right mood to savor the pleasures of visiting Japan because we just wanted to get home. And so we spent our first three days in Tokyo eating western food. Tokyo has the best pizza in the world.

Chapter 4

Marx, Money and Mysticism after Mao

Marx:

There is a zero-risk method that we Americans can use to end human rights abuses in China. We can point out the fact that the cruelty of Marxism comes from the writings of Marx. We can do it here, among ourselves. Everything that is said in America gets heard in China.

The authority of the Chinese Communist party is based on the respect that all Chinese people feel for Marx. They may love capitalism. They may have no interest whatsoever in political theory. But they believe that Marx was always right and always good. The only reason that Marxism failed, they think, is the evil of human beings. The government of China can command the loyalty of the citizens because it is the heir of Karl Marx.

In America, nobody—left, right or center—ever stops to consider the possibility that Marxism comes from Marx. If only we could talk about how destructive it is to look forward to the world Marx envisioned, a society with no disagreement, China would hear us and understand us.

An old story used to circulate in the Soviet Union: Once there was an emperor who was very evil and very fierce. He said $2 + 2 = 6$. All the people were afraid of him and agreed that $2 + 2 = 6$.

When the emperor died the next emperor was less evil and less fierce. He said $2 + 2 = 5$. All the people asked themselves, "How could we have been so stupid as to believe that $2 + 2 = 6$?"

A young mathematician thought for a long time. He concluded $2 + 2 = 4$. He wrote a book to prove his theory. He decided to take it to the publisher, but on the way, two strangers approached him. "Comrade," they asked, "what are you doing? Do you really want to go back to the days when 2 and 2 were 6?"

The story applies better to contemporary China than it ever did to the Soviet Union. Chairman Mao was the first emperor. The leaders who have ruled since Mao, most notably Deng Xiaoping, are the second emperor. The mathematician who dared to think the unthinkable was the multitude who sat in Tiananmen

Square for six weeks in 1989. And the two strangers who told the mathematician not to rock the boat are the apparent majority of the citizens of China.

Marxism encourages sacrifice for the public good. There is no awareness of the fact that what is good for the public is the sum of what is good for each person. There is no recognition of the rather obvious fact that people will always disagree, not simply because their interests may clash, but because different individuals view things in different ways. Human life could not have survived without both selfishness and altruism. In Chairman Mao's day, the government and the people spoke only of altruism; today they speak only of selfishness. The second is the negative of the first, but both views are equally simpleminded and equally wrong.

Democracy is the institutionalization of the fact that disagreement is both inevitable and good. Marx didn't distinguish between democracy and other political systems. In the *Manifesto*, he wrote, "Political power, properly so called, is merely the organized power of one class for oppressing another." He was wrong. A philosophy that looks forward to the end of conflict of interest leads logically and inevitably to a society where disagreement is viewed as the embodiment of evil. When individuality was outlawed, individuals themselves were considered worthless. Countries as different as Russia, Ethiopia, and China all developed the same architecture, the same "neighborhood committees," the same fear of thought. What is even worse, they pursued policies that led to starvation on a catastrophic scale. Such a famine is currently taking place in North Korea. It is no accident, comrade.

When we got back to America a week after the Tiananmen Massacre, all our Chinese friends in New York were pro-student and anti-government. Things have changed. Many of my friends who were pro-student in 1989 have since decided that Deng Xiaoping did the right thing in crushing the demonstration. Someone I know who acted courageously during Beijing Spring no longer supports the movement he had risked his life for. I haven't been back to China, but people I know who have gone there tell me that public opinion in China has changed as well. Now people seem to be saying they want stability, not democracy. They remember the days of the Cultural Revolution, when gangs of Red Guards entered people's homes searching for books, paintings or musical instruments, all of which were illegal at that time. They say that they need stability to prevent a return of the Red Guards. Somehow they don't realize that it was Chairman Mao himself who invented the Cultural Revolution and inspired the Red Guards. There are very few people in the world who know that democracy is the most stable form of government.

Money:

Deng Xiaoping said, "To get rich is glorious." Friends and former students I knew in China who have visited the United States recently have told me that nothing is more beautiful than money, and that they are interested in money, not politics. "Compact affordable car revs up for sale," says a front-page headline in the December 13, 2000, issue of *China Daily*, an English-language newspaper published in Beijing. At least some people in China are indeed getting rich.

In the days of Chairman Mao, nobody talked about money. It was assumed that what was good for a particular person was necessarily bad for the People. The world was viewed as a zero-sum society where good luck for an individual was considered bad luck for the masses. Self-interest was thought to be anti-social—especially if money was involved. The People was at war with people.

This view grew out of the line in the *Communist Manifesto*: "The history of all hitherto existing society is the history of class struggles." In a class struggle, there are class enemies, and Chairman Mao had divided people into the *hong wu lei*, the five red (good) categories—workers, soldiers, peasants, revolutionary martyrs, and Communist Party officials—and the *hei wu lei*, the five black (bad) categories—landlords, rich peasants, rightists, counterrevolutionaries, and bad elements. No one wanted to risk being classified as rich and therefore a member of one of the five black categories.

The acceptance of the legitimacy of wanting to be rich is perhaps the biggest change in China since the death of Mao. Everywhere in the world, people want to be rich. Money is needed not only for food, clothing and shelter but for education, culture and comfort. Nevertheless, there is something weird about the slogan, "To get rich is glorious." It is a reflection of the inversion of a society where people used to believe that poverty is virtue. Deng Xiaoping kept the old Marxist system intact but turned it upside down. China today believes in capitalism with the same religious faith that it once applied to its belief in communism. Marx, in *The Communist Manifesto*, tells us that the bourgeoisie "has left no other nexus between man and man than naked self-interest, than callous 'cash payment.'" Yet it is China today that glorifies naked self-interest and does not allow other connections among people to exist.

China's current system has been described as market Leninism. That is a misnomer. Market Leninism is what Taiwan had in the days of Chiang Kai-shek. The Nationalist Party, the Kuomintang, was openly Leninist in its structure and adopted the Leninist principle of "democratic centralism," which means strict obedience to the party (see Jonathan Spence, *The Search for Modern China*, p. 338). What China has today is Marxist capitalism: the belief that nothing matters but economics—not culture, not individuality, not biology, not politics. Marxist capitalism is Marxism with a minus sign in front of it.

Mysticism:

What is a religion? Each religion defines the word "religion" in a different way. Confucianism teaches a way of life and accepts an order in the world, but Confucius was vague about the nature of the gods. Is Confucianism a religion? This is not an easy question. Taoism is generally recognized as China's indigenous religion. Yet the philosophy of Lao Tzu, the founder of Taoism, is independent of belief in the supernatural. Buddhism was China's major religion before 1949, yet among the Han people, the ethnic Chinese, Buddhism seemed to be about ritual rather than ethics. All societies have religious traditions, but one might argue that China was the least religious of traditional societies.

Perhaps this fact makes China a country whose citizens are likely to get swept up by new systems of belief. There isn't enough old religion to form an alternative to the rapid rise of a new faith. In 1836, a man living in Guangdong Province named Hong Xiuquan became a Christian. After having many visions, he concluded that he was the son of God and therefore the younger brother of Jesus Christ. He founded the Taiping Movement, which was both religious and political, and between 1850 and 1864, a bloody civil war was fought between the Taipings and the government of China.

Marxism too is a system of belief, although an explicitly atheistic one. In the days of Chairman Mao, faith in Marxism was absolute. Marxists believe that there are inevitable stages of history: primitive communism, feudalism, capitalism, socialism, and the final stage of communism. When this final stage comes, there will be no economic inequality and therefore no conflict of interest, since the only cause of disagreement is money. The state will then wither away.

Chinese people today say they no longer have any interest in Marx. They simply want to get rich. Yet their acceptance of money as the sole source of happiness shows that Marxism has conditioned their patterns of thought. Other habits of thinking introduced by Marxism remain. Love of money hasn't necessarily changed the view that the poor are good and the rich bad. Marxism, ironically, has prepared China to accept some of the teachings of the Sermon on the Mount: "Blessed be ye poor: for yours is the kingdom of God. Blessed are ye that hunger now: for ye shall be filled. Blessed are ye that weep now, for ye shall laugh. But woe unto you that are rich! for ye have received your consolation. Woe unto you that are full! for ye shall hunger. Woe unto you that laugh now! for ye shall mourn and weep" (Luke 6:20-25).

Arthur Waldron, writing in the Spring 1988 issue of *Orbis*, reports the following information:

> Numbers of Protestant Christians in China have climbed so dramatically that their officially sponsored organization has had to scramble to accommodate even its own members. Thus, foreign visitors who wished to join Protestant worship in Beijing in the 1970s were regularly taken to a lovely small chapel with an adjoining parsonage for the minister, who was always happy to meet them. A decade later, however, the chapel was far too small, and what looked to be a vast old octagonal revival hall on the campus of a school was pressed into service. This is not to mention the numerous house churches, where unofficial Christian groups gathered, or the revival of indigenous Chinese Christian sects, such as the True Jesus Church (which now has converts and churches in foreign countries as well).

> Roman Catholicism has shown similar vigor. Because of their loyalty to the pope, Catholics were persecuted relentlessly during the 1950s and 1960s, foreign missionaries were expelled or imprisoned, and Chinese clergy were murdered or sent to the gulag.

There is a large Catholic church in the heart of downtown Baoding. In 1984, mass was still celebrated in Latin. We knew an elderly faculty member at Hebei University who was a Catholic. He never went to that church. I later found out the reason: the downtown church belonged to the Patriotic Catholic Association,

China's official pro-contraception, pro-abortion Catholic Church. A devout Roman Catholic would not go there.

We personally had no problems connected with religion in China. On Purim, both in 1984 and 1989, we invited students and colleagues to our apartment, where we all took turns reading from the Book of Esther—in English. Our Chinese guests didn't know the story, and all of them cheered at the end. There was another American family at Hebei University in 1984, the Lewises, nonobservant Protestants from Minnesota. They didn't know the story either, and were quite upset to learn that when the villain, Haman, was hanged, his sons were executed as well. Our celebration of Purim deepened our knowledge of the differences between American and Chinese culture.

After Purim of 1989, a student came and asked me if he would be invited to our Passover seder. The question surprised me, but we had in fact brought matzohs and haggadahs with us to China. I told him that we would invite friends on the faculty to the first seder and graduate students to the second, but we just didn't have room for our 80 or so undergraduate students. "Last year Miss Ruth invited the undergraduates," he said.

We got to know a Muslim colleague at Hebei University during our first stay, in 1984, and he invited us to services at the local mosque at the end of the month of Ramadan. It was the first time I had seen an Islamic service. I should add that in 1984 we also attended Presbyterian services at a house in Baoding that was used as a church. On our second visit, in 1989, we attended Buddhist services in Shanghai and Inner Mongolia, which we visited during our spring break. The Lamaist Buddhist Mongolian worshippers looked more devout to me than the Han worshippers in Shanghai, but I must add that one can't judge devoutness by looking at people while they pray. China does not accept the idea of freedom of religion, but those forms of religion that are not considered threatening are functioning freely. $2 + 2 = 5$. Other groups, of which the Roman Catholic Church is the best known, are not allowed to worship. $2 + 2$ does not yet equal 4.

We never attended a Marxist service in China; strictly speaking, there is no such thing. What there was instead were required political meetings for faculty and students at Hebei University, and someone we knew said they were like church. When my wife asked why, he answered, "They are boring." Perhaps I should have asked whether I could attend, but I didn't. I am told that there are no more required political meetings in China.

China recently cracked down on a spiritual group called Falun Gong, which, clearly, is considered threatening. I know almost nothing about the beliefs of this group, but its ability to mobilize lots of protesters at short notice is already a threat to the government. It is not clear whether Falun Gong is considered dangerous because of its dogma or because it is an example of civil society.

After Mao:

An enormous change that has happened in China is the appearance of labor unions. An article in the December 14, 2000, issue of *China Daily* entitled "Unions vital to workers' rights" tells us, "Trade unions are being urged to mobilize workers nationwide to help consolidate achievements made through the reform and development of State-owned enterprises," which sounds as if the unions are a tool of the government. Nevertheless, the article goes on to say that "trade unions should also focus on safeguarding the interests and rights of workers by fashioning a more effective mechanism to solve the problems of laid-off workers and workers' rights violations." Can it be that China is actually allowing citizens to organize? It's hard to believe. That would be tantamount to recognizing that individuals and particular groups have rights that are not the same as the rights of the People.

Life is freer than before. The first time I taught in China, in 1984, one never saw a boy and girl walking together. Once, a student of mine asked me the secret of America's wealth and power, and I answered "freedom." "But if we had freedom, it would lead to sex," he said. Today there is more freedom, and it has led to sex. Not only that, it has led to divorce. An article in the February 23, 2000, issue of *China Daily* appeared under the headline, "Bear it or leave it: Divorce a suitable solution for sinking marriage." According to the article, the increase in divorces may lead to a new law making divorce harder.

Because of China's one-child policy, there are a disproportionate number of boys in the country. China values boys more than girls, partly because boys are responsible for the care of their elderly parents. Pregnant women would sometimes have an amniocentesis and then decide to abort the fetus if it was a girl. More boys have been born than girls. These boys are growing up. There will not be enough women for them to marry.

Perhaps this gender disproportion is the reason for China's new attitudes toward homosexuality. Or maybe it is just part of a world-wide development that has reached the Chinese public despite limits on freedom of the press. Both these factors may be at work. Be that as it may, China's official English-language newspaper, *China Daily*, reported on August 17, 2005, that Shanghai's prestigious Fudan University was offering a course on tolerance for homosexuals. The news article also mentioned that sodomy had been decriminalized in 1997 and that in 2001, homosexuality had been struck off China's list of mental disorders.

More recently, on September 6, 2005, an article discussed the prejudices faced by homosexuals. And on November 11, 2005, there was a headline that read, "Gays in Guangdong show unity and pride," accompanied by a photograph of a young man named Zheng Yuantao and a caption saying "Proud to be gay." Despite the fact that *Brokeback Mountain* is not being shown publicly, a news story in the February 12, 2006, edition of *China Daily* entitled "New book shows different aspects of gay life" refers to *Brokeback Mountain* as touching. Furthermore, Tong Ge, the author of the study referred to in the headline, is cited as saying "reading this will help people know gay men as normal human beings instead of patients to be analyzed."

On December 19, 2005, there was another news item in *China Daily* that went even further. The headline read, "Proof: it's not always a man's world," and the message of the article was that men may choose sex-change surgery and become women.

The acceptance of homosexuality, to say nothing of sex-change operations, is a gross violation of Marxist theory. Marx never mentioned homosexuality, but he believed that all differences among humans were the result of economic factors. Individual differences, according to Marx, will disappear when the final stage of communism arrives and a classless society exists, when one will "hunt in the morning, fish in the afternoon, rear cattle in the evening, [and] criticize after dinner" (*The German Ideology*).

In the days of Chairman Mao, there could not be anything resembling civil society; all loyalty was to the state and the Communist Party. There was no loyalty to one's friends and family. Reporting relatives and neighbors for being rightists or counterrevolutionaries was common. In the Soviet Union, Pavel Morozov—a child who was murdered by his neighbors after he reported his father for supplying food to starving kulaks, the analog of "rich" peasants, one of the five black categories—was a national hero. China had no publicly honored equivalent of Pavel, but one of my students, Xue Wen, told me that his mother had reported his father for having counterrevolutionary thoughts. The father died in jail. A second student, a month or so later, told me that Xue Wen had turned in his mother for the same crime. I knew Xue Wen's mother, who seemed to be on good terms with her son. I never asked Xue Wen about this.

There is no more reporting of family members, but there still is no civil society—no independent groups, formal or informal, and no sense of public responsibility independent of the government. But China still honors Karl Marx, who hated civil society. He described it in the dirtiest words he knew: "It is from its own entrails that civil society ceaselessly engenders the Jew" ("On the Jewish Question"). In other words, civil society is so ugly that it excretes Jews from its bowels.

Trevor Corson, who studied at Beijing Normal University in 1989, wrote in the February 2000 issue of *The Atlantic Monthly*, "The origins of the movement among Chinese students were less romantic, and less clearly about democracy per se" than Western reporters believed. My own impressions of that time were that there was great interest in democracy and in political theory. People asked me wonderful questions about separation of powers and about the rule of law. It was in China that the May 4th Movement arose in 1919, a movement that chose "Science and Democracy" as its slogan. It was in China that people first understood that democracy—arguing, testing, reconsidering—is the political realization of the scientific method.

Even though the Chinese are no longer interested in Marx, the legitimacy of the Communist Party is based on the unquestioning respect that people have for Marx. If Americans won't say bad things about Marx, why should the Chinese be different? On the other hand, if we and they can see just how much Marx opposed democracy, we can all live in a world where $2 + 2 = 4$.

Chapter 5

China, Marx, and Islam

In 1972, the Japanese Red Army Faction sent a suicide squad to Lod Airport in Israel to kill Jews. Half the people they killed turned out to be Puerto Rican Christian pilgrims, but since the Red Army Faction volunteers were willing to die in order to fulfill their goal, they probably would have been willing to kill non-Jews as well in order to complete their mission.

Perhaps these members of the Japanese Red Army Faction were the first suicide killers in the Middle East. We associate suicide bombing with Muslim fanatics, but Marxists can be equally fanatic. Marxists may be atheists but they have faith, which is what unites them with Islamists.

This unity dates back to the Bandung Conference, held in Indonesia in 1955, when a de facto Marxist-Islamic alliance was formed. Bandung took the world by surprise. Earlier in 1955, before the conference took place, it had seemed likely that Israel and China would exchange ambassadors. In 1949, Israel was the sixth non-Communist nation to recognize the People's Republic of China. Anson Laytner, in "China's Israel Policy Reviewed" (*Middle East Review*, Summer 1989), writes: "In January 1955, an Israeli Trade and Goodwill Mission spent 20 days in China. A five-point protocol agreement was signed on February 28. . . . However, China's slowness in agreeing to send a reciprocal delegation to Israel and the Israeli Foreign Ministry's fear of antagonizing the Eisenhower Administration led Israel to delay its decision. . . . The next month, at the Bandung Conference, Chinese Premier Zhou Enlai and the Chinese delegation first met with Egyptian President Nasser, Palestinian leader Shukeiry and other Arab leaders. Immediately afterward, on April 29, 1955, Israel advised China that it sought full diplomatic relations. But it was already too late" (p. 55).

For most of its history, the People's Republic of China viewed its interests in purely ideological terms. In fact, in order to eliminate class differences, Chairman Mao was actually willing to close high schools and universities for ten years during the Cultural Revolution (1966 - 1976). After Bandung, anti-Zionism became a central, albeit unstated, part of communist ideology. What had begun as a practical act—a political coalition with Islamic nations—continued even after it was no longer practical. When capitalist-roader Deng

Xiaoping took over, ideology was ignored except where free speech was concerned; Israel, therefore, could do business with China. On the other hand,
diplomatic recognition could not come until the Berlin Wall fell and Eastern
European countries recognized Israel—and got away with it.

The Third World, which is heavily Islamic, has been China's ally and spiritual companion. Does this alliance have anything to offer China today? China no
longer respects poverty; the people and the government are united in their scorn
for backwardness and what they call "superstition." The ideological component
is weakening, but the oil remains. Yet it is easy to imagine conflicts of interest
between China and Islam. On February 25, 1997, a bus explosion in Xinjiang
Province, home of the Uighurs, who speak a Turkic language and are Muslims,
killed nine people and injured 57. If a separatist or pan-Islamic movement
gained strength in western China, it might gain world-wide support, which
would be more threatening to China than the sympathy that already exists for
Tibetan independence.

If ever there were to be a post-Marxist China, suspicious of both religious
and political dogma, it would spontaneously ally itself with a relatively secular,
post-Enlightenment country like Israel rather than with the Third World. As for
oil, it is very much in Israel's interests to discover alternative sources of power.
Israel has long been a leading force in the use of solar energy.

When I went back to China to teach at Hebei University during the spring
semester of 1989, my own students were among those demonstrating in
Tiananmen Square. I felt I saw Marxism as an intellectual system die before my
eyes. Indeed, within a few months, Communist regimes had been overturned in
country after country. In China, however, where 1989 began, the ghost of Marxism continues to rule, alas.

The ghost of Marxism remains alive in the West as well. Karl Marx is still
honored even though socialism is considered a failure. Leftists—those who worship the ghost of Marx—hate America. America is the land of civil rights,
women's rights, and gay rights. Leftists don't know this. They support these
rights, but are de facto allies of radical Islam, despite the honor murders of
women and homosexuals in Islamic countries.

The political institutions of the Western world arose from the thinking of an
era called the Enlightenment or the Age of Reason. Reason was obviously not
invented in the 18th century; what is significant about that period in history is
that reason became a political issue. The idea of political freedom was a logical
outgrowth of a belief in reason, since the politics of reason depends on the freedom to reason.

Karl Marx did not consider himself a mystic, and the philosophy he created
was consciously committed to rationality. Yet Marxism has a definite mystical
component. Marxists believe that capitalism is doomed, although there is no
evidence to support such a belief. Stranger yet, they believe the state will wither
away, although few states were ever less designed to wither than communist
regimes. They even believe that alienated labor and conflict will end all by
themselves once communism is achieved. If that is not mysticism, what is?

Marxism, like any human phenomenon that exists through time, has evolved. It has been modified by Leninism—and by its own power. What started out as a system concerned with economics and achieving a classless society has developed into a doctrine concerned with maintaining and extending its influence. Its goal is orthodoxy.

Before 1989, there were probably only two systems of belief left in the world that people would kill for: Islam and Marxism. Now there is only one: Islam. Deng Xiaoping, the last leader to kill for Communism, ordered the Tiananmen Massacre because he wanted the Chinese to believe in Marx. The struggles between religious communities in Bosnia, Kosovo, and Northern Ireland immediately come to mind, but the troubles in these places are national rather than religious struggles, though the nationalities are defined by religious affiliation. In the 21st century, killing for one's nation is widespread; killing for one's belief is restricted to the world of blind faith. During the troubles in Northern Ireland, nobody ever planted bombs to argue for the truth of transubstantiation versus consubstantiation. The citizens of Ulster, like those of Bosnia and Kosovo, fought for the control of their country, not to propagate their beliefs.

To a certain extent, we live in a post-Marxist, post-Jewish, post-Christian world. It is true that there are many countries (Israel and the Republic of Ireland are examples) where the dominant religion is powerful; it is even true that in China, Cuba, and North Korea the official faith can never be challenged. Only Islam, however, has never faced widespread agnosticism and indifference. It is impossible to find a believer in Judaism so fervent as to advocate stoning for adultery or a Catholic so devout as to believe in a revival of burning at the stake. It is even hard to find a Marxist who believes that struggle sessions and purge trials should return to China and Russia. But there are Islamic countries where both adultery and heterodoxy are punishable, and on occasion, capital offenses.

Muslims and Communists waged a bloody war in Afghanistan for several years. Islamic states have jailed Marxists; Communist countries have persecuted Muslims. Nevertheless, for a long time, there has existed an implicit Marxist-Islamic alliance. It operates in votes at the United Nations and in acquiescence or complicity in international terrorism. Leftist writers now feel free to attack Stalin and Mao, and maybe even Castro, but they remain blind to the excesses of Islamic regimes. For example, the Left has still not faced the fact that Khomeini's revolution in Iran and the victory of the Taliban in Afghanistan, now partially undone, set back the rights of women more than any other event in any country in recorded history. During the first Gulf War, American leftists claimed they supported the relatively secular regime of Saddam Hussein over the orthodoxy of Saudi Arabia, but Hussein's strident anti-Zionism and anti-Americanism were what really linked him to the left. After that war Saddam Hussein became more openly pro-Islamic; nevertheless, he did not lose any support among secular leftists.

The alliance still survives. North Korea has sold weapons to Iran. "Egypt's military relationship with North Korea goes back to the early 70s, when Pyongyang sent an air battalion to Egypt as a sign of solidarity in its war with

Israel," according to an article by Eli J. Lake and Richard Sale in the June 22, 2001, issue of the *Middle East Times* entitled "U.S. Worries over Egypt-North Korea Missile Program." More recently, the *London Review of Books*, a leftist journal, ran a series of letters in its October 4, 2001, issue expressing varying degrees of hostility to the United States after the events of 9/11. Perhaps the most egregious was a letter by Eric Foner, an otherwise intelligent scholar of American history, who wrote, "I'm not sure which is more frightening: the horror that engulfed New York City or the apocalyptic rhetoric emanating daily from the White House."

Marxism was strong—and Islam still is—for a variety of reasons. Each is a complex system of analysis, supported by a wealth of intellectual tradition, which can explain every aspect of human life. To the educated, these philosophies offer a framework; to the simple, they offer the security of always knowing what is right and wrong. These positive strengths are supported by a great fear, the fear of a phenomenon perceived as evil: personal freedom—especially sexual freedom, and most particularly pornography and homosexuality. In addition to this great fear, there is a great obsession—an inordinate concern with an issue that really should not merit very much attention: Zionism.

Few societies have ever tolerated free sex. One of the functions of societies is to provide for the rearing of the next generation, which in most communities of the world has involved fathers taking responsibility for their offspring—a responsibility much more easily evaded when it is unclear who has fathered whom. Kinship systems form a key part to any social order. Perhaps it makes biological sense for the human species to place social limits on the free indulgence of our biologically determined sexual desires. Not surprisingly, a great number of philosophical and religious traditions have defined sexual freedom outside of certain clearly specified family situations as sin.

In the industrialized West, these restrictions began to break down even before the widespread availability of contraception. In the late 1960's, a real sexual revolution took place in the United States and much of Europe. The obvious reason was that the risk of unwanted pregnancy had been greatly reduced. A second and less obvious reason is that sexual freedom, when accompanied by easy access to contraceptives, works to control population. Unmarried partners living together are less likely to have children than married couples. Homosexual acts do not lead to pregnancy. In a modern society in which population control is a desideratum, sexual freedom is socially useful.

In a religious world, sin is sin, and no amount of social desirability can change that. It doesn't matter whether or not religious believers are interested in population control. Fundamentalist nations necessarily look upon sexual freedom as evil. The West is not only sexually free, but rich and powerful. Its movies spread its values everywhere. Its comforts and luxuries tempt the world. It is not hard to understand why Khomeini thought of the United States as the Great Satan. The wealth of American society and the promise of pleasure offered by American personal freedom threaten to undermine one of the most central of religious prohibitions. America is not hated because it is Christian but because it is free. Despite this fact, anti-American leftists, feminists, and gay rights activists remain blind to the persecution of women and homosexuals in Islamic countries.

Communism, like all forms of blind faith, is opposed to sex even though leftists in non-Communist countries are likely to be much more sexually liberated than their apolitical compatriots. The Soviet Union went through a brief period of encouraging sexual freedom, but that was before totalitarianism had succeeded in intruding into private life. In China, puritanism used to be as strong as it is anywhere in the world. To a certain extent this is true because of traditional Chinese values, but to a greater extent it is the consequence of Marxist suspicion of personal freedom. Leftists have always remained silent about the anti-sexual policies of Marxist regimes.

China is desperately concerned about the size of its population. It has embarked on a one-child policy. Until recently, no one in China was aware that there is a connection between the sexual liberation of the West and its relatively low rate of population increase. Even if the awareness had been there, it would not have made any difference. China was a determinedly anti-sexual society under Chairman Mao. Now that Chairman Mao is dead and the Cultural Revolution has ended, China has begun to accept the idea that it is all right for people to pursue happiness.

During the periods I lived in Baoding, I had expected that there would be people who told me that America had no freedom, that our elections were rigged, our thoughts controlled by propaganda, and our liberties meaningless. I had certainly heard statements to that effect back home, both from Americans and occasionally from foreign students. But to my surprise, no one in China ever suggested to me that they thought Americans were not free. Some envied us our liberty or even said they desired it for themselves. The more common attitude in 1984 was that China was better than the United States because America was being destroyed by the perniciousness and emptiness of freedom, which was an expression of our acquisitiveness and had led to crime, disintegration of the family, and a society in which friendships existed only for economic reasons.

The essence of this negative view of freedom was that in America there was rampant sex. I was asked (with a certain amount of hesitation and apology, since no one wanted to embarrass me) whether it was true that there was pornography in America. I acknowledged that there was. I was also asked whether there was homosexuality. When I suggested that homosexuality was a practice that should be permitted in a country that was trying so hard to keep its population down, no one could understand how I could possibly think of something so outlandish. I was told that there was no homosexuality in China, that there never had been and never would be. The items cited from *China Daily* in the previous chapter show that things have changed. It was hard to explain that in the United States families do exist, that most people have very little contact with pornography, and that divorce is frequently better than no divorce. When I said that I thought China would be a more prosperous country if people were free to choose their jobs or express their political opinions, the standard response was that Chinese society would disintegrate if freedom were tolerated.

When I went back to China in 1989, I never heard anyone say that freedom might lead to sex. There had already been student demonstrations, which had begun in Hefei, in Anhui Province, in December of 1986, and spread to Shanghai, Beijing, and elsewhere. Clearly, there were many Chinese who longed for freedom and democracy. They wanted an escape from the drabness of communism as well; consequently, their apartments were more colorful, their clothing brighter, and sometimes their hair (men and women both) curled.

It is not clear whether China and repressive countries in general are afraid of freedom because it might lead to sex, or whether they are afraid of sex because it might lead to freedom. In 1989, there were restrictions on personal choice that many people in China found painful: one could not choose one's place of residence or one's job. Consequently, many married couples were separated, sometimes for decades, when they were assigned jobs in different cities. This was an extraordinary policy for a nation that prides itself on the stability of its families. Nevertheless, no one protested against this policy, mostly because protest is not allowed in China, but also because there is no real acceptance of the idea that people have a right to make individual choices, even about so personal a question as whether they may live in the same part of the country as the rest of their family.

China, to be sure, has embraced capitalism, which one might think is an even greater violation of Marxist theory. But Marx said that the final stage of communism would have to be preceded by feudalism, capitalism, and socialism. Chairman Mao ignored Marx when he tried to jump from feudalism to socialism without going through capitalism. China nowadays is correcting Mao's heterodoxy by passing through the inevitable capitalist phase of history. China's leaders know that socialism and communism must come eventually, since they believe that Marx can never be wrong, but they hope these changes will not occur within their own lifetimes.

In the days of Chairman Mao, it was illegal to own a dog in a Chinese city. The reasons were unclear, but a state that demands total love cannot allow dogs to compete with it for affection.

Chairman Mao is dead and China has changed, somewhat. A headline in the October 10, 1994, edition of China Daily reads, "Dog question becomes hottest topic in capital." The article reports that an annual registration fee of 6000 yuan ($700) will be required of dog owners in Beijing. China's current administration values money more than love. Another crack has opened.

China has learned something that Marx said was unthinkable: people are different from each other. The cracks will continue to widen. Freedom will enter.

On the other hand, China's opposition to Zionism remains. This is actually quite a curious phenomenon. Both Israel and China have used a woman driving a tractor as a national symbol (it was never a true representation in either country); both are places where, for a long time, it was never necessary to wear a necktie.

There is neither an ideological nor a practical reason for hostility against Israel to exist. Honest people may honestly disagree about Zionism, as they may on any number of issues. But no one could seriously believe that Israel is any kind of threat to any Communist state. Nor is it possible to think that Israel is in some way a danger to Marxist ideology. Despite the accomplishments of its defense forces, its military situation is inherently precarious.

Its most controversial policies in recent years, the existence of checkpoints, the invasion of Lebanon, and the destruction of houses while searching for terrorists by the Israeli Army in places like Jenin and Gaza, are considered by many people to be examples of injustice and violence, but they are minor wrongs indeed when compared to Cambodia's auto-genocide, the Iran-Iraq War, China's conquest of Tibet, Indonesia's massacre of ethnic Chinese, ethnic cleansing in Bosnia and Kosovo, the violent repression of the Chechens by Russia, or the genocide in Darfur. On the other hand, even the most fervent of anti-Zionists will concede that Israel has achieved a remarkable degree of civil liberties for a country that has never been at peace.

Israel's handling of the Al-Aqsa Intifada drew worldwide condemnation. But if there had not been an Intifada, or if Israel had managed to deal with it in a gentler fashion, Israel would not have been any more accepted by the world community today. Indeed, it was during Israel's attempt to cope with the first Intifada that the UN rescinded its Zionism-is-racism resolution. The revolt of the Tamil Tigers in Sri Lanka is in certain ways parallel to the two Intifadas, but it has been very much more bloody. More than 3,500 rebels, security forces and civilians were killed in the second half of 1990 alone (reported in *China Daily*, January 12, 1991). Whether the government could or should have exercised more restraint is open to debate. Equally debatable is the relative justice of the opposing sides. Nevertheless, Sri Lanka remains an accepted member of the family of nations. Incidentally, Sri Lanka is the only non-Marxist, non-Islamic nation that voted to retain the Zionism-is-racism resolution.

Sri Lanka is a small and unimportant country, and what happens there is of little direct interest to outsiders. Israel too is a small and unimportant country, a fact no one seems to have noticed. Anti-Zionism is so strong and so widespread that Israel's marginality remains undiscovered.

Despite Israel's lack of importance and despite the weakness of the moral charges against it, Israel is an outcast. Israeli nationalism—Zionism—has been declared racism. The Arab League enforces secondary and tertiary boycotts against Israel. Jews may not enter Saudi Arabia, except for American soldiers. Malaysia forbids the performance of "Jewish" music. This endless policy of boycott and non-recognition is officially the policy of most Arab states. Countries like Libya, Iraq or Saudi Arabia have never suggested that they would make peace if Israel did X or Y or Z. Their opposition to Israel, supported by leftists everywhere in the world, is one of permanent enmity. Since such a stance excludes the possibility of peace, it is implicitly genocidal and therefore radically evil.

Anti-Zionism is one of the great hatreds of our time. Why do Marxists and post-Marxists join in this extremism? One reason is lack of originality, a common failing in countries with no structure for the expression of opposition. Marx and Lenin died before the creation of Israel and so could not have written about it. The pair of anti-Semitic essays Marx wrote under the title, "*Zur Judenfrage,*" provides a theoretical reason to oppose any form of Jewish power and might explain the situation, despite the fact that few people care about this work and even fewer have read it. What seems to have happened was first Bandung and then a period shortly before the beginning of the Six-Day War, when anti-Zionism became a primary part of Marxist doctrine and has remained so through inertia. In other words, Marxism is anti-Zionist because it has defined itself as anti-Zionist.

Russia and China now have diplomatic relations with Israel. Shedding Marxist dogma leads automatically to the abandonment of anti-Zionism. On the other hand, those few remaining American leftists who are still fighting the Cold War remain anti-Zionist, supported Saddam Hussein, and root for an American defeat in Iraq.

Islam's anti-Zionism is less surprising than the hostility that is found among Marxists. After all, Jerusalem, the third holiest city for Muslims, is now in Israel. Yet before the Six-Day War, East Jerusalem, which is where the holy sites are located, was in Jordan. Arab anti-Zionism was no weaker then than it is now. Before 1948, Jerusalem was ruled by Great Britain. Anti-British sentiment among Islamic peoples has occasionally been strong, but never has it had the ferocity of anti-Zionism. The establishment of Israel led to a refugee problem and ultimately to the creation of Palestinian nationalism. These factors are not so much the causes of anti-Zionism as the result of it. The United Nations Partition Plan of 1947 was an attempt to create both a Jewish and an Arab state. The Jews then living in Palestine accepted the idea of a Palestinian Arab state; the Arabs rejected it because of their anti-Zionism.

Most people know that between 1948 and 1967, Jews were not allowed to visit East Jerusalem. Fewer know that during the same period, Israeli Muslims did not have the right to do so either. What is even more shocking is the fact that until 1977, Israeli Muslims were forbidden by Saudi Arabia from fulfilling the religious obligation of making the *hajj*. It was more important to the Saudis, the guardians of Islam's holiest places, to deny the existence of Israel than to let fellow Muslims obey their religion. In other words, being anti-Zionist had in effect become a more important part of Islamic law than Islamic law itself.

Suicide is against Islamic law. Amir Taheri, in an article in the *New York Post* issue of April 20, 2003, entitled "The Truth About Jihad," writes that for Muslims, suicide is an unpardonable sin, "in the same category as denying the Oneness of God." Yet devout Muslims everywhere cheer suicide bombers who die so that they can kill Jews. Once again, we see that anti-Zionism has become a more important part of Islamic law than Islamic law itself.

Former President Ali Akhbar Hashemi Rafsanjani of Iran, according to Memri Special Dispatch Series No. 325, in the annual Al-Quds (Jerusalem) sermon given on December 14, 2001, said that if one day the world of Islam came to possess nuclear weapons Israel could be destroyed. The use of a nuclear bomb against Israel would leave nothing standing, but any retaliation, however severe, would merely damage the world of Islam. For Rafsanjani, damage doesn't matter, since there is no cause more important than anti-Zionism. Rafsanjani today is called a moderate, since President Ahmadinejad has been much more explicit in his call for Israel to be erased from the map.

Who needs more enemies? Saddam Hussein, during the first Gulf War, facing the active enmity of the United States, at that time the leader of a coalition of 28 nations officially or actually at war with Iraq, launched SCUD missiles against Israel's population centers, in order to tempt an extra army to fight against him. The courting of new foes ought to surprise us, even in this irrational world we live in. No one is puzzled at all, however. We all know the reason: Iraq wished to divert attention from its unpopular invasion of Kuwait by espousing a popular cause: anti-Zionism.

There are any number of solutions to the problems of the Israelis and the Palestinians. Unfortunately, Arabs who attempted to find such solutions— President Sadat and King Abdullah are the best-known examples—have been assassinated. It is not in the interest of the Palestinians to remain forever homeless and persecuted. The Palestinians can advance their interests only with the Israelis, not against them. They have not yet done so, because the thought of accepting Israel's existence—a rather obvious fact—is more horrible to them than the thought of being attacked and massacred by Jordanians, Lebanese Christians and Shiites, Syrians, or Kuwaitis.

If anti-Zionism is one of the great hatreds of our time, that is no doubt because it is the child of anti-Semitism, one of the great hatreds of history. Nevertheless, it is neither logical nor practical. It survives because it is not questioned. If it were not for anti-Zionism, Islamic fundamentalism would be weaker. Arabs could dare to say that there is a way to live in peace with Israel.

Irrationality did not die with Marxism. Nationalism is as fierce as ever. Religious fighting in India, a danger that seemed remote for decades, is once again a threat to life and peace. Blind faith, whether political or religious, places restrictions on thought. It is therefore a denial of the greatness—indeed, the essence—of the human species. Blind faith is what links Islam to the ghost of Marxism.

Chapter 6

Happiness in Chinese Culture

"Happy? Happy is when you don't have a broken leg, so far as I know," says May Wynn, a character in Herman Wouk's *The Caine Mutiny*. In other words, happiness is the absence of serious unhappiness. Western culture has always found unhappiness easier to describe than happiness. When we consider ancient Greek drama, the tragedies of Sophocles and Euripides move us today; the comedies of Aristophanes, however, are not especially funny. In Chapter 28 of the Book of Deuteronomy, the blessings that God will give His people if they obey His commandments are straightforward examples of everyday life: rain in its season, for instance. The curses if the people disobey are lengthy, imaginative, and poetic, like the following: "And the Lord will bring you back in ships to Egypt ... and there you shall offer yourselves for sale to your enemies as male and female slaves, but no man will buy you" (28:68).

Dante's *Divine Comedy* is another example of how much easier it is for Westerners to talk about misery than about happiness. The *Inferno* is hellish because it is close enough to our experiences on earth for us to comprehend; the *Purgatorio* is the same, albeit a temporary hell; the *Paradiso* is vague, difficult to grasp, and somehow not heavenly at all.

Chinese philosophers, on the other hand, don't have too much to say about misfortune. Confucius, the best known and most influential thinker in Chinese history, wrote about *rén*, meaning "benevolence" or "virtue." This word, perhaps not by coincidence, is a homonym of the word meaning "human" or "person," although it is written with a different character, composed of the elements "person" and "two." To be both human and benevolent is to be humane; the concepts are linked linguistically in English as they are in Chinese.

Confucius believed that virtue could be achieved through *lǐ*, which means both "ritual" and "courtesy." Ritual was important to Confucius despite the fact that Confucianism is not a religion. There is a gap between Chinese philosophy and faith, reflected by a similar gap between ritual and belief. Although religious ritual plays an important role in Chinese culture, Chinese civilization stands out among the world's ancient traditions as having no place for religious faith.

Taoism, spelled Daoism in the *pinyin* system of Romanization used in Mainland China, is generally considered a religion. Its founder, Lao Tzu (Laozi in *pinyin*), accepted the world the way he found it, with all its complexity and contradictions. He taught that one should follow the *dao*, the way, the path. Jewish law, incidentally, is called *halakha*, which also means "way" or "path." Jewish law, however, is detailed and precise; the *dao* is unknowable. "The *dao* that can be told of is not the eternal *dao*," according to the opening verse of the *Tao De Ching*, or *Daode Jing* in *pinyin*. Among the many cryptic statements we find in the writings of Lao Tzu is the following:

> Banish sageliness, discard wisdom
> And the people will be benefited a hundredfold.
> Banish humanity, discard righteousness,
> And the people will return to filial piety and affection. (Chapter 19)

Lao Tzu was the first post-modernist. Everything is true and false at the same time. "To seek learning one gains day by day; to seek the Tao one loses day by day." (Chapter 48) How would Lao Tzu define happiness if he were willing to give an answer that could be understood? I think he would say the following: Take it easy. Don't try too hard. Don't try to figure things out. Enjoy good luck. Enjoy bad luck.

Confucius, on the other hand, did not delight in paradox. What delighted him was life: learning, exploring, music, ritual, courtesy, respect, etc. "In education there are no class distinctions," he said in the *Analects*. (15:38) He is famous for his statement about disagreeing with one's parents:

> In serving his parents, a son may remonstrate with them, but gently;
> when he sees that they do not incline to follow his advice, he shows
> an increased degree of reverence, but he does not abandon his pur-
> pose; and should they punish him, he does not allow himself to
> murmur. (4:18)

In other words, Confucius was trying to reconcile independence with obedience. Instead of accepting paradox, he called for subtlety. He also called for being humane: "A man who is not humane, what has he to do with rites? A man who is not humane, what has he to do with music?" (3:3) He was interested in this life, not the world to come: "We don't know about life, how can we know about death?" (11:11)

When asked if there was a single word to sum up what one's conduct in life should be, Confucius answered "reciprocity" and illustrated what he meant by saying "Do not do unto others what you would not want others to do unto you." (15:23) This is a negative phrasing of the Golden Rule. It appears across cultural lines. In the Book of Tobit in the Apocrypha, we read, "Do not do to anyone else what you hate." (4:15) Rabbi Hillel expanded on it when he said, "What is hateful to you, do not do unto your neighbor. All the rest is commentary, go forth and learn." Confucius agreed. Would he have agreed with the positive phrasing used by Jesus in the Sermon on the Mount? Jesus said, "Therefore all things whatsoever ye would that men should do unto you, do ye even so to them: for this is the law and the prophets." (Matthew 7:12) We can't know what Confucius would have thought about this verse, but we do know what George Bernard Shaw thought. He says, in the "Maxims for Revolutionaries," appended to his play *Man and Superman*, "Do not do unto others as you would that they should do unto you. Their tastes may not be the same."

Confucius and Lao Tzu disagreed about reality, about striving, and about virtue. Nevertheless, they viewed the world as a happy place. They loved life and they loved people. A different Chinese philosopher, Hsün Tzu (Xunzi in *pinyin*), had a relatively negative view of humanity: "The nature of man is evil; his goodness is acquired." (Chapter 23) Hsün Tzu was not talking about original sin. Instead, he was calling for education. Man, said Hsün Tzu, "must submit himself to teachers and laws before he can be just; he must submit himself to the rules of decorum and righteousness before he can be orderly."

The philosophers I have referred to lived a long time ago. Confucius is believed to have lived from 551 to 479 B.C.E., before Socrates, Plato, and Aristotle. Lao Tzu is traditionally believed to have antedated Confucius. Hsün Tzu lived from 298 to 238 B.C.E. Long before any of them wrote, however, Chinese was a written language. Chinese is written in characters which began as simplified pictures. Eventually, the characters became logographs—signs for words. That is what they are today. Sometimes a character has two or more elements, one of which is often a radical, which tells us something about the meaning, while the other may be a phonetic, which tells us something about the sound. The radical and the phonetic are themselves characters or variants of characters. Thus, two or more characters can be put together to create new characters.

To illustrate this, let us consider two characters, one pronounced *fù* (falling tone), meaning "wealthy"; the other pronounced *fú* (rising tone), meaning "happiness." The characters are similar in having a complicated phonetic representing the sound *fu*. The character for "wealthy" has a roof over the phonetic. The roof suggests wealth, among other things. The character meaning "happiness" has a symbol to the left suggesting ritual. The combination of ritual and the sound *fu* suggests happiness, or at least did when the characters were created. The phonetic has three elements: the number one, a mouth, and a field. The meaning of the combination of these three elements may also suggest happiness or wealth. Happiness is good fortune. Wealth is a fortune. The English words "fortune" and "fortunate" reflect a linking of these concepts.

All languages have synonyms: words with the same meaning, but not exactly. In English, we have "joy," "gladness," "contentment," etc. In Chinese, another word for "happiness" is *lè*. The character for this word is the same as the character for *yuè*, meaning "music." The sound of these two words is different today, but the fact that they are written in exactly the same way suggests that they once were the same word. Chinese writing tells us that music is the same thing as happiness.

Still another synonym is *xǐ*. It suggests delight as well as happiness. At a wedding, we see this character doubled. Double happiness is clearly linked with marriage in Chinese. The divorce rate in China is going up, as is happening in

many parts of the world, but a marriage is still double happiness. In a movie by
Ang Lee entitled *The Wedding Banquet,* this character appears three times in the
opening credits—triple happiness. The movie is about a *ménage à trois,* three
people, a woman and two gay men, living happily together after one of the men
marries the woman. The extension of the double-happiness symbol is an interesting example of the evolution of both language and culture.

Delight, marriage, good fortune, music. These associations are even older
than the ideas of virtue, courtesy, learning, order, and acceptance that we find in
Chinese philosophy. In every single case, however, happiness is the appreciation
of the world. Even Hsün Tzu, who said people are evil by nature, said that by
nature they want to be good and can become good.

Then came Buddhism, which reached China in the first century C.E., according to tradition. China under the Han Dynasty was going through a difficult
period. The Han Dynasty finally collapsed in 220, and a period of disunity followed. Perhaps that was a factor in leading Chinese thought from its optimistic
acceptance of reality to a religion that, like most religions, recognizes the uni-
versality and power of suffering. Buddhism teaches that one is reincarnated from
one painful life to another. What one hopes for is Nirvana, when there will be no
more reincarnations. Somehow, Buddhism and Confucianism coexisted, although they seem to contradict each other.

Buddhism reached its peak during the T'ang Dynasty (Tang in *pinyin*),
which lasted from 617 to 907. The Tang period produced a number of famous
poets, among them Li Po (Li Bai in *pinyin*), who wrote a very well-known poem
about the joy of drinking with his friends: the moon and his shadow. We may
interpret the poem differently, as the tragedy of being driven to drink with no
human friends. Whatever our reading, the poem does not reflect Buddhist spiri-
tuality. It may be closer to the Taoist tradition of finding happiness—the
mysteries of the Way—in the apparent contradictions of life. A later Tang poet,
Po Chü-yi (Bai Juyi in *pinyin*), who lived from 772 to 846, was rather political.
Here is a poem about free speech, translated by Arthur Waley:

> Sent as a present from Annam—
> A red cockatoo.
> Colour'd like the peach-tree blossom,
> Speaking with the speech of men.
> And they did to it what is always done
> To the learned and eloquent.
> They took a cage with stout bars
> And shut it up inside.

Politics is an attempt to improve society, which arguably shows that Bai
Juyi was following the version of Confucianism expressed by Hsün Tzu: we are
bad but we can achieve happiness by working to become good.

Buddhism was arguably the religion of most of China's people for almost
two millennia; nevertheless, Chinese culture has never been especially spiritual.
Ancestor worship has been identified as China's religion, although it is not part
of any system of theology. Christianity appeared in the late 16th century. A mis-

sionary named Matteo Ricci finally succeeded in meeting the Emperor in 1601. Some Chinese were converted, but the numbers remained small. Then in the 19th century, a village schoolteacher named Hung Hsiu-ch'üan (Hong Xiuquan in *pinyin*) received visions telling him that he was the younger brother of Jesus Christ. Perhaps the visions really meant half-brother, with Hong and Jesus sharing God as their father but with different mothers. He established Taiping Christianity. Taiping means "great peace" and is the name of the Pacific (or "peaceful") Ocean. Hong prohibited opium, tobacco, gambling, alcohol, prostitution, extra-marital sex, and foot binding. Women were officially equal with men. The Taipings were considered anti-Confucian because of both their puritanism and their advocacy of women's rights. A bloody war broke out, which ended in a horrible massacre in 1864. The Taiping Rebellion may have been the strongest revolutionary movement in Chinese history up to that time.

What was happiness for the Taipings? They combined mysticism with politics and self-denial with a program to aid the poor and the oppressed. They wanted justice in this world and salvation in the next. Confucians, who believed in education, discussion, self-improvement and the reality of the world, might have been expected to be revolutionaries, but they weren't. Confucians and Taoists were happy with the world; they were not willing to risk revolution to improve it. Buddhists, who looked forward to the end of the cycle of reincarnation and Nirvana, did not believe happiness could be achieved through life. The Taiping Christians, who believed true happiness could only be found in heaven, felt that one had to be moral on earth in order to achieve salvation. They created a revolution to improve life as part of the road to happiness after life. They combined a program of justice and equality with sternness and intolerance. They believed in brotherhood, yet they destroyed Taoist and Buddhist sculptures, which they considered idolatry. Chairman Mao admired Hong Xiuqian. Mao and Hong both rejected the idea of happiness in the short run.

China fought on the side of the side of the Allies in World War I. When Germany was defeated, China expected that parts of Shandong Province that had been occupied by Germany would be returned. Instead, the Versailles Conference awarded Germany's former possessions to Japan. Many students at Beijing University rioted on May 4th, 1919. That was the beginning of a period of political activity and intellectual dissent know as the May 4th Movement. The Movement's slogan was "Science and Democracy." It is somewhat surprising that nobody had noticed that science—testing, examining without restrictions, reconsidering old theories—is in effect just what democracy does. Democracy is the political realization of the scientific method. On the one hand, May 4th was acting in the Confucian tradition of learning. On the other hand, holding demonstrations was very much a contradiction of the Confucian idea of respect. The May 4th Movement was anti-Confucian, yet it was at least in part following the Confucian belief in the reality of the world.

There is a May 4th Street in many Chinese cities. May 4th is a minor holiday, called Students' Day. Chairman Mao did not feel threatened by a philosophy that called for science and democracy, which is quite surprising, since he was opposed to both science and democracy. He closed down high schools and universities during the Cultural Revolution (1966-76) and exiled teachers and scholars to the countryside so that they could learn from the peasants. He suppressed free speech as it had never been suppressed before, encouraging people to report their friends and relatives for counterrevolutionary thoughts. Parents feared their children, and with good reason. A careless remark heard by a child might get repeated to someone else, and the parent could be arrested for being a rightist. Some children actually denounced their parents to the authorities. China was no longer the land of filial piety.

In place of the Confucian ideals of courtesy, benevolence, and reciprocity, Mao introduced thought reform, *sixiang gaizao*. Everyone in a Marxist society would be equal economically, which was supposed to mean that everyone would have the same interests and therefore think in the same way.

What about happiness? Happiness was to be achieved through loving the Communist Party, loving China, and loving Chairman Mao. Service and sacrifice to the ideals of Marx and Mao were the only legitimate forms of happiness. Theater and opera were banned, except for the revolutionary operas selected by Mao's wife, Jiang Qing.

And certain pets were banned. City dwellers were not allowed to own dogs. Those who had dogs had to give them away to a farmer or allow them to be killed. They could be eaten afterwards. The reason, never stated and perhaps never understood by those who created this prohibition, was that love is finite. Citizens should not squander love that ought to be directed to the Communist Party on their own pets.

Nowadays, this law had been modified. China today is preoccupied with money. An ID for one's dog can be purchased for a large sum of money. According to the September 20, 2004, edition of *China Daily*, in the city of Xi'an, an ID used to be 5,000 yuan ($600), but it has been lowered to 500 yuan ($60). Apparently the city officials could not collect enough money with their high fees, and so they lowered them.

China has entered the stage of Marxist capitalism. Marx wrote that humanity had to pass through a number of stages: primitive communism, feudalism, capitalism (during which science and technology would be discovered), socialism, and the final stage of communism, post-technological and therefore rich. Chairman Mao thought he could skip the capitalist stage. China's current leaders have rejected Mao's heterodoxy and accepted capitalism as a necessary period society must go through. They know that communism must come eventually, since they believe Marx can never be wrong. But they hope it will not come during their own lives. However, they really aren't thinking about Marx, although they are influenced by his analysis. Marx taught that nothing matters but economics. Therefore, nothing is more important than money. Nowhere in the world do people talk about money more than they do in China. Today, happiness means money, period.

The strength of Marxist capitalism is illustrated by news stories and op-ed essays in China's government-controlled press. *China Daily* ran a headline on February 22, 2005, announcing "Income gap grows wider in Beijing." It is a bit hard to think of a country run by the Communist Party announcing such news.

Even more surprising was an op-ed on February 19 entitled, "Let the market fully play its role." The author, Zhou Tianyong, is a researcher at the Party School of the Central Committee of the Communist Party of China. The essay suggests that the government of the People's Republic should "bring out the role of the market in allocating resources and clarify the rights of production factors." This doesn't sound like a People's Republic. It sounds like the Republican Party.

There is another tendency, however. Religion is making an appearance. An organization called *Falun Gong* (law-wheel exercise) or *Falun Dafa* (law-wheel big-law) has spread in China and is being persecuted by the Chinese government. It teaches *qigong* breathing exercises, an aspect of Taoist ritual. It is a modern expression of Taoism, China's oldest organized religion. Christianity is spreading as well. Various Protestant denominations are growing, and new Chinese versions of Christianity are being created, although they are less innovative than the Taiping Christianity of the 19th century.

Both love of money and religious faith are post-Marxist phenomena in China. Love of money exists everywhere, but in China it is the heir of the Marxist teaching that all motivation is economic. Religious faith exists everywhere, but in China it is the heir to the atheistic faith of Marx, who taught that the world would inevitably go through its pre-determined stages of history. Furthermore, the Marxist commitment to thought reform facilitates the unquestioning acceptance of dogma.

Will China ever return to the Confucian identification of happiness with virtue and reciprocity? Will China ever seek happiness through the May 4th identification of democracy with science? Only time will tell.

Part II

Reconsiderations

Chapter 7

Reconsidering Marx

Marxism has been rejected around the world. One reason for this is the fact that Marxist nations everywhere were trapped in backwardness. As the world's living standard advanced, Communist countries remained poor. The gap became increasingly visible with time. A second reason is that Marxist states have been unusually brutal. In a world whose history is the story of cruelty, nations ruled by the Communist Party stand out among the most vicious. Stalin, Mao, Pol Pot, Castro, Mengistu, Ceaușescu—it can't just be a coincidence.

Karl Marx, on the other hand, has not been rejected anywhere. His writings are studied, cited, and loved in the West and the East, by academics, historians, and even theologians. Nevertheless, the key to understanding this cruelty can be found in the writings of Marx and Engels.

Marxism is the negation of both science and reason. Marx asserted, with no evidence whatsoever, that human history is a series of inevitable stages: primitive communism, feudalism, capitalism, socialism and communism. It is most peculiar that a man who didn't believe in God could believe that the course of history was predestined. Marx had no understanding of the necessity for disagreement. In his vision of the final stage of communism, the state would wither away because without class differences, there would be no conflict. What nonsense. If there are human beings, there will be thought. If there is thought, there must be disagreement. If there is disagreement, there must be some form of government to keep the peace.

For Marx, all motivation is economic: there is no culture, no personal preference, no love, and no desire to learn. Therefore, the only possible way people can be selfish is over money. In a communist society, Marx thought, there could not possibly be any selfishness, since there would be no class conflict.

The boundary between selfishness and altruism, however, is not as clear as Marxists think. Every individual has personal, family, neighborhood, professional, national, and world interests. All of these are simultaneously selfish and altruistic. Each of us belongs to many smaller and larger circles at the same time. Every group has different needs, all of which are valid. What is advantageous for someone's family, for example, may not be in the interests of the town. One may experience conflict between one's roles of family member and citizen, which is not to say that one of these roles is somehow more moral than the other. For Marxists, however, those interests that coincide with the goals of the working class and the class struggle are automatically altruistic; all others are selfish.

Marx was opposed to the idea of civil society. In his essay "On the Jewish Question," he said, "*Practical need, egoism*, is the principle of *civil society*, and is revealed as such in its pure form as soon as civil society has fully engendered the political state. The god of *practical need and self-interest is money*" [emphasis in original].

What civil society really means is a set of rules—some enforced by law, others by custom—to enable large and complex societies to function peacefully and honestly. In villages, where everyone knows everyone else, society functions through personal obligations. Roles in a pre-capitalist society are clearly defined by age, sex and class; when one person helps another, it is understood that the favor must be repaid. An urban, modern society cannot function merely through respect for one's superiors and the repayment of favors. Such a society inevitably leads to corruption. That is precisely what exists in China. Obedience to those in authority is no substitute for law. A system of mutual obligation is no substitute for a legal system in which rights are spelled out. Unfortunately, in countries ruled by the Communist Party, the Party itself is above the law. That is quite consistent with Marx's dismissal of civil society and his view that the state would wither away.

Corruption is found in the West too; no place on earth can be totally honest. However, the problem is less acute in democratic countries. Democracies can establish the concept of personal rights and universal rules, which apply to everyone and not just to one's friends. Governments and businesses alike can function in the Western world free from the weight of corruption; Communist societies, which dismiss the idea of human rights as just another example of selfishness, cannot protect themselves against corruption.

Marxism, which rejects the ideas of rights and civil society, cannot recognize that there are natural conflicts that arise among the legitimate needs and desires of different people. If all discordant needs are merely selfish and therefore immoral, these needs are to be stamped out, Marxists say, rather than regulated and incorporated into civil society. But there are certain needs that cannot be stamped out. When basic needs cannot be satisfied legitimately, they will be satisfied illegitimately. When there is no front door, there will be a back door.

Marxism not only engenders corruption, it also protects it. In a free society, the press is always looking for scandals. In a political system with more than one party, each party is looking for ways to embarrass the other parties. When people look, they find. Corruption is constantly being uncovered and eliminated. In a country where Marxism rules, on the other hand, there can only be one party, since disagreement is not legitimate. There cannot be a free press, since freedom would allow room for an anti-communist press. And so there is no press and no opposition to perform the vital role of exposing corruption.

Corrupt societies are necessarily poor; honesty is needed to enable business to function. Yet if all corruption disappeared tomorrow, Chinese society would not be any better. China's greatest tragedies had nothing whatever to do with corruption. Chairman Mao was not corrupt. Neither were the Red Guards. The reason they were so bad was precisely because they were not corrupt; they believed in what they were doing. Human beings are at their most cruel when they think they are acting for a cause that is more important than mere life. Mao Zedong, like Hitler, was able to cause the deaths of millions because he thought he was doing good. Mao had nothing personal to gain when he exported grain in the years 1959 to 1961, during the greatest famine in all recorded history, a famine in which 35 million people may have died. He did it because he wanted to achieve instant industrialization, in order to prove the superiority of Marxism. Nor was Mao acting selfishly when he launched the Cultural Revolution. He did it because Marx had said there would be no distinction between the city and the countryside when communism was finally achieved. He did it because Marx had said that there would be no professionals, and therefore no intellectuals, in the final stage of communism.

Chinese people find it very hard to understand that Mao's cruelty did not arise from personal selfishness. They have been taught Marxism so long that they cannot comprehend the existence of non-selfish motivation. Moreover, it is easier to think that Mao was bad than to admit that Marxism itself is the problem.

Every Marxist leader has been extraordinarily cruel. Stalin, Mao, Ceausescu, Pol Pot, Mengistu, Castro, the Kims—is it all just a coincidence? Marxism has to be just exactly what it has been wherever it has been tried—a system that leads to uncontrolled barbarism.

In China, children denounced their parents as counterrevolutionaries; husbands divorced their wives for being rightists. "In China we love our families," say the Chinese. "In capitalist countries there are no family ties because people love only money," they say. And they believe it.

In China, vicious Red Guards terrorized the population; citizens jeered and mocked their friends and neighbors at struggle sessions. "Marxism teaches kindness and sacrifice," say the Chinese. "In capitalist countries there is no humanity, just love of money," they say. And they believe it.

Marxism led to cruelties on the personal level that had no precedent in Chinese history. Yet all its excesses are blamed on a few bad individuals. Not only did Marxism make the Chinese bad; it made them stupid.

In order to become good and intelligent, the Chinese people must embrace science, or in other words, adopt a democratic system of government. By democracy, I do not simply mean the rule of the majority; I mean freedom of speech, freedom of thought, separation of powers, and the rule of law. The Tang-Dynasty poet Li Bai (Li Po) believed in freedom; so did Li Zicheng, who overthrew the Ming Dynasty in 1644; so did the May 4th Movement. There is nothing foreign about democracy; science and truth are universal. Marxism, however, is an alien ideology that was adopted by China.

It doesn't matter whether the economic system is socialist or capitalist. Indeed, China has encouraged the introduction of markets for over a decade. The Communist Party does not object to the practice of capitalism as long as the people believe in socialism. That is because Marxism is not an economic system; it is a religion about an economic system. Talking about politics as if the only variables were economic systems is a mistake that comes from Marx. The way to revitalize China will come through politics, not through economics. There is no substitute for democracy. Democracy is a commitment to the pursuit of truth, and to find truth, there must be the freedom to think.

Despotism is as old as history. Tyrants may simply seize and hold power through the use of force, or they may claim to rule by divine right. The twentieth century, during which liberty has advanced further than ever before, has ironically produced the most repressive of all forms of despotism: totalitarianism. Hannah Arendt, in *The Origins of Totalitarianism*, claims that fascism, Nazism and communism constitute a qualitatively different form of tyranny, which tries to achieve not only absolute obedience but thought control as well.

Thought reform was an explicit goal in the days of Mao Zedong and remains so today, although the words themselves, *sixiang gaizao* in Chinese, have fallen out of favor. Chairman Mao claimed that all power comes from the barrel of a gun, but he ruled not only through force but through something akin to divine right: he was revered not only as an individual but as the symbol of the inevitable triumph of Communism. It is ironic that fascism, Nazism and communism—all atheistic philosophies—by their commitment to thought control defined heresy as a punishable offense. Indeed, totalitarianism has usurped the place of religion, which is one of the ways it differs from simple despotism. Traditional religion is suppressed because there can be no alternative to the new official faith of the state.

Another irony is the fact that these twentieth-century doctrines reject the twentieth century in favor of the vision of a pre-lapsarian past. For communism, this ideal situation was an imagined era of primitive communism; for fascism, it was Ancient Rome; for Nazism, a time of racial purity. In every case, the past represents perfection because it is viewed as uniform, containing no discordant elements, and thus a time when individuals did not have their own personal needs or desires. Every totalitarian ideology has demanded absolute service to the ideals of the system. This devotion was equated with selflessness and viewed as the essence of morality. Murder and betrayal for the cause were equated with goodness.

Fascism and Nazism were defeated. Everywhere in the world, these ideologies are now seen as the embodiment of radical evil. Since the fall of the Communist Party in eastern Europe and the old Soviet Union, socialism is generally described as a system that didn't work. Nevertheless, communism, or its ghost, still rules a billion people in China.

The Cold War is over, and capitalism is spreading throughout the former Soviet bloc. China, however, whose population is more than double that of what used to be called the Soviet bloc, still believes in Marx. Yet China is having a love affair with capitalism, euphemistically called "socialism with Chinese characteristics." A free-market economy is growing rapidly in China, but neither China's leaders nor its citizens consider this a rejection of Marx. Rather, it is a return to the original theory, which said a society has to pass through capitalism before reaching the socialist stage. It was Mao Zedong who rejected this theory by trying to jump from the feudal stage directly to socialism.

Liberals used to be called "soft on Communism." Yet all Marxist regimes have curtailed freedom, tried to control thought, imprisoned or executed dissidents, and in general devoted their energies to enforcing orthodoxy. Marxism, wherever it was in power, was a profoundly anti-urban doctrine. Yet Marx and Engels lived after the Enlightenment and were considered radicals. It is a paradox that their teachings have led to a rejection of thought, science and questioning.

Marx and Engels dreamed of a world that embodied all the values of the primitive, tribal society—of the Noble Savage. They imagined a world without merchants and therefore without commerce. It was a world without inequality and therefore without experts or professionalism. And yet this dream was the creation of highly sophisticated urban writers who felt that the revolution they were calling for would be made by the urban proletariat. There is an internal tension in Marxist theory that cannot be resolved—the contradiction between the sweet, bucolic dream they believed would be realized and the complex, urban structure that had shaped them and enabled them to formulate this very dream.

The dream was called "the higher stage of Communism" by its creators and was described in Section 1 (a) of "Feuerbach" in Marx's *The German Ideology*: ". . . in communist society, where nobody has one exclusive sphere of activity but each can be accomplished in any branch he wishes, society regulates the general production and thus makes it possible for me to do one thing to-day and another to-morrow, to hunt in the morning, fish in the afternoon, rear cattle in the evening, criticize after dinner, just as I have a mind, without ever becoming a hunter, fisherman, shepherd or critic." When the "higher stage of Communism" is achieved, the state will wither away, according to Engels. In Chapter 9 of *The Origin of the Family*, he tells us that the state "has not existed from all eternity... The society that organizes production anew on the basis of free and equal association of the producers will put the whole State machine where it will then belong: in the museum of antiquities, side by side with the spinning wheel and the bronze axe."

This dream is not simply impossible; it is a nightmare. Its ugliness comes from its rejection of the human desire to know more and more, which involves specialization; from its denial that people want to move from the country to the city and not vice versa; from its blindness to the fact that disagreement is inherent in human nature and necessary if society is to change and face new problems. Moreover, believing that this impossible situation is one's goal is dangerous because it involves a commitment to believing a lie and a consequent abandonment of rationality. In order to protect the lie, the state must be designed to eliminate the freedom to examine the philosophy underlying this lie.

What is communism? The nation states that we think of as communist refer to themselves as Marxist-Leninist. According to Chapter II of the *Communist Manifesto*, communism "may be summed up in the single sentence: Abolition of private property." Then it would seem that the kibbutzim in Israel should be called communist.

Before I lived in China, I thought of communism as a destructive and mistaken analysis of the human condition. After I lived there, I learned it is not an analysis at all, but rather a dark and horrible religion. The first time I lived in China (February to July 1984), everything I saw led me to believe that communism is not an economic system but a faith about an economic system. The purpose of the Chinese government is to teach that faith, but not necessarily to follow the teachings. All departures from Marx's teaching were explained by saying that China was a socialist country and that communism, i.e. "the higher stage of communism," had not yet been achieved. Therefore bankruptcy laws and the incentive system were not violations of communism but merely steps along the road.

In the short run this hypocritical point of view has led to liberalization, an increase in living standards, and a booming economy. Yet in the long run there is something extremely dangerous about "the higher stage of communism," since it implies an attempt to recreate human nature through propaganda and force.

Lenin, in Chapter 5 of *The State and Revolution*, says that "The State will be able to wither away completely . . . when people have become accustomed to observe the fundamental rules of social life, and their labor is so productive, that they voluntarily work *according to their ability*. . . . Until the 'higher' phase of Communism arrives, the Socialists demand the *strictest* control, *by society and by the State*, of the quantity of labour and the quantity of consumption" [emphasis in original]. Lenin's words sound hypocritical and contradictory: strictest control seems a peculiar way to arrive at a stage where there is no control. Unfortunately, there is no contradiction. The "strictest control" called for by Lenin is needed because human nature would have to be altered in order to produce the society he envisions, otherwise people might not "voluntarily work according to their ability." Indeed, such a stateless world would be unchanging and without strife, or else government would have to reappear.

The Marxist vision of the future implies the realization of a society without disagreement and therefore the end of history. That is why thought reform is a considered a desirable and realizable goal. Those societies that have attempted to reshape human nature have been noted for their ruthlessness. All of the cruelty of Communist states, all of the evils committed by Stalin, Mao and Pol Pot, are implicit in the Marxist idea of the withering away of the state.

One consistent aspect of this cruelty was an attack on city dwellers. Pol Pot emptied the cities; Mao exiled millions to the countryside. Chapter II of *The Communist Manifesto* lists ten measures for revolutionizing the mode of production. The ninth of these is the "combination of agriculture with manufacturing industries; gradual abolition of the distinction between town and country, by a more equable distribution of the population over the country." This is entirely consistent with the vision of an ideal life when one would "rear cattle in the evening [and] criticize after dinner."

The official reason that people were forced to live in the countryside during Mao's Cultural Revolution was so that they could learn from the peasants. What was it that the peasants were supposed to teach them? China's antiquated agricultural techniques? Of course not! City people were supposed to learn how to become members of a society with relatively little change. The most permanent of human institutions are found in rural areas. If Mao wanted to achieve the dream of ending history, he had to make everyone think and act like peasants. What the Cultural Revolution was trying to do was to make China a land where all the citizens would accept their lot without questioning. Peasants, especially in poor countries, know that life is hard and nothing can be done about it. Urban dwellers know a different reality—that the world is growing ever more prosperous.

Mao Zedong was not upset by the fact that the Cultural Revolution was causing nothing but hardship and reaction. He had no vision of a better life for the Chinese people. His *Little Red Book* deals with only two issues: how to win and how to punish one's enemies after winning. Once Mao had achieved victory and eliminated his enemies, what was there left for him to do? He had no further program. All he could do was punish the Chinese themselves. Yet despite Mao's inability to imagine a better life for China, he believed in Marxist theory. He wanted a China that would never again have another revolution—a China in which history would have ended. Rural China, in certain respects, resembled a society in which history had never begun. Mao was ready to lead China from feudalism to communism without ever going through the intermediate stage of capitalism. He did not need an urban proletariat; his revolution had already taken place. It is not surprising, then, that Mao's contribution to Marxist thought was his elevation of the peasants to a revolutionary class.

Communism under Mao was very much like feudalism. In both these systems, the overwhelming majority of the population is equal and powerless. At the top, there is a tiny, highly structured class. In medieval Europe, this was called the nobility, and consisted of titled ranks (duke, earl, etc.) with the king, who ruled by divine right, at the top of the pyramid. In China, those at the top were called *cadres*. Like the nobility, they are ranked, not by title but by number. There were 23 degrees of cadres. And at the top was the absolute ruler, Chairman Mao. In both systems, there was a faith that could not be questioned, since heresy was punishable by death. And both systems were based on the assumption that nothing would ever change in one's lifetime. In feudal Europe, one had to die to go to heaven. In China, paradise was the higher stage of communism, which was eventually to be reached on this earth. But for those who died before the higher stage of communism was achieved, there would never be any heaven at all.

The second half of the 20th century was a period of great social change. In China, however, attitudes are extremely conservative. China has no tradition of a single religion that is the repository for conservative attitudes. Instead, it is Marxism itself that has been the tool of resistance to social change. In fact,

Chapter I of the *Communist Manifesto* deplores the fact that history moves so quickly in bourgeois societies: "All that is solid melts into air, all that is holy is profaned, and man is at last compelled to face with his sober senses his real conditions of life and his relations with his kind." Since Marx and Engels are calling for revolution, it is startling to realize that they understood just how revolutionary capitalist society can be: "Constant revolutionising of production, uninterrupted disturbance of all social conditions, everlasting uncertainty and agitation distinguish the bourgeois epoch from all earlier ones."

Mao's China was hardly a bourgeois society, yet it was a time of "uninterrupted disturbance of all social conditions." Just as Lenin advocated "strictest control" in order to make the state wither away, Mao exiled city dwellers, split families and encouraged the Red Guards to wreak havoc in order to build a rigidly unchanging world. Most Chinese people, who equate Marxism with goodness, prefer to think that Mao's excesses were not related to Marxist ideology; they would rather believe that he was merely interested in strengthening his own political position. Perhaps he was. Nevertheless, he was a good Marxist who instinctively understood that the "higher stage of communism" meant a world without change and without cities.

Like fascism and Nazism, communism rejects cities as it rejects intellectuality and complexity. Marx was a monist. For him there was one explanation for any social, personal or political problem: the class struggle. There is no psychology, no sociology, no anthropology; there is only economics. Much of what Marx and Engels had to say is counterintuitive. *The Communist Manifesto* notwithstanding, it is not at all obvious that "bourgeois marriage is in reality a system of wives in common." Nor does it seem accurate to say that "national differences and antagonisms between peoples are daily more and more vanishing." Furthermore, it is difficult to conceive of urban life without trade, but Engels informs us in Chapter 9 of *The Origin of the Family* that there is no need for commerce: "Under the pretext of relieving the producers of the trouble and risk of exchange . . . a class of parasites was formed, real social bloodsuckers, who as compensation for very slight actual services skimmed the cream off both home and foreign production. . . ."

There is a possibility that Marx's analysis is not nonsense. A theory that is counterintuitive does not have to be wrong. Investigation, observation and debate—all dangerous activities in a communist country—could possibly show that the elaborate analysis constructed by Marx has some validity. But the whole theory seems to be based on ridiculous assumptions: that all value comes from labor, that all motivation is economic, that there is no altruism in capitalist societies. If this were so, there would never have been support for communism among the intellectuals and bourgeoisie of the West. Furthermore, Marxism has not made life better. China did not produce anything beautiful under Mao—no music, no literature, no architecture. Communism did not even end hunger. An article about the famine of 1959-1961 appeared in the December 1985 issue of *Scientific American*. The author, Vaclav Smil, informs us, "More detailed demographic data released by the Chinese since 1981, together with the results of the 1982 census (which was by far the most reliable Chinese census), put the number of excess deaths in that period at 30 million and the number of lost or postponed births at about 33 million. No other known famine has been so devastating."

The second time I lived in China, during China Spring (1989), everyone seemed to be totally in agreement with the student protests. Yet many people were uncomfortable with the thought that Marx could have been wrong. They said that his ideas were created in a different time and place and were not entirely relevant; they granted that Marxism in China had been influenced by feudalism; they agreed that Marx had been misinterpreted. What they could not do was question the essential correctness of his thesis. They continued to excuse the evils of the past and the harshness of the present by saying that China had not reached the "higher stage of communism." They continued to view this fantasy of the future as possible. Worst of all, they considered this vision of mindlessness and obedience as something positive.

It is possible and usually quite interesting to view the world from a single perspective. If Marx explained everything in terms of the class struggle, Freud did so in terms of the unconscious, and Jesus did so in terms of salvation. A monistic theory may be enlightening, but it does not take into account the complexity of life. Furthermore, Marx and Engels were unconvincing when they wrote about the uselessness of merchants or the end of the division of labor. A flawed theory can still be useful if it is recognized as a theory. But when it becomes doctrine—when it is to be believed under penalty of law—then it changes from a theory into a lie. Marxism in China is just such a lie. No one seems to understand that there is a relationship between the enforcement of belief in a lie and the feudal thinking that China has not succeeded in eliminating.

Totalitarianism—a form of despotism that attempts to control everything, even thought—is always anti-Semitic. Jews, for better or worse, have given the world such earth-shaking thinkers as Moses, Jesus, Marx, Freud, and Einstein. Jews are trained from childhood to argue, to think dangerous thoughts. The more a philosophy discourages thought, the more it persecutes the Jews.

Feudal societies in Europe were characterized by reflexive hatred of the Jews. Obscurantist societies are by their nature intolerant. Marx shared this ancient prejudice. Not only is his early work, *On the Jewish Question*, filled with negative generalizations about Jews, so is his *magnum opus*. The following quotations, from Chapters 1, 4, and 5 respectively of Volume I of Marx's *Capital*, all refer to Jews:

> Trading nations, properly so called, exist in the ancient world only in its interstices, like the gods of Epicurus in the Intermundia, or like Jews in the pores of Polish society.

> The capitalist knows that all commodities, however scurvy they may look, or however badly they may smell, are in faith and truth money, inwardly circumcised Jews, and what is more, a wonderful means whereby out of money to make money.

> The sum of the values in circulation can clearly not be augmented by
> any change in their distribution, any more than the quantity of the
> precious metals in a country by a Jew selling a Queen Anne's far-
> thing for a guinea.

It is impossible to understand what Marx is saying about Jews in these quotations since he is not saying anything at all. The statements are simply
gibberish. We can gather that his feelings are hostile and that he cannot keep
them down. But he does not explain what is bothering him. Let me venture a
theory. Jews are the most urban of groups. Marx hates them because he hates
modern society. Jews are intellectuals. They think too much.

For Marx, the supreme sin was capitalism. Needless to say, he blamed the
Jews; since Jews did not rule Europe, he claimed that Christianity had been "re-
absorbed into Judaism": "It was only then [after Christianity was reabsorbed]
that Judaism could attain universal domination and could turn alienated man and
alienated nature into alienable, saleable objects, in thrall to egoistic need and
huckstering" ("On the Jewish Question").

There is no place for those who think too much in the "higher stage of communism," and there is no place for diversity. Thinking may lead to change. It is
no accident that good revolutionaries were especially likely to be among Stalin's
victims. Nor is it a coincidence that Party members were likely to be attacked by
Mao and his Red Guards. Revolutions eat their own children.

In villages, where everyone knows everyone else, society functions through
personal obligations. Roles in a pre-capitalist society are clearly defined by age,
sex and class; when one person helps another, it is understood that the favor
must be repaid. An urban, modern society cannot function merely through respect for one's superiors and the repayment of favors. Such a society inevitably
leads to corruption. That is precisely what exists in China. Obedience to those in
authority is no substitute for law. A system of mutual obligation is no substitute
for a legal system in which rights are spelled out. Unfortunately, in countries
ruled by the Communist Party, the Party itself is above the law. That is quite
consistent with Marx's dismissal of civil society and his view that the state
would wither away.

Communists and anti-Communists, Easterners and Westerners, persist in
arguing that Marxism has never really been tried. After more than 70 years, after
similar patterns of indoctrination and suppression in countries as different as
Cuba, China and Belarus, will nobody consider the possibility that Marxism
comes from Marx?

Marx said that "national differences and antagonisms between peoples are
daily more and more vanishing." He was wrong. He said the value of a product
is the value of the raw materials plus the value of labor. He was wrong; such a
product is worthless if nobody wants it. He said that there had been no merchants in ancient times. He was wrong; he had never heard of the Silk Road. In
fact, as long as 2,600 years ago, merchants regularly traveled as far as 5,000
miles. Marx was wrong about everything.

Chapter 8

Reconsidering Salvation through Faith

Jesus is perhaps the most influential philosopher who ever lived. His words are familiar even to non-Christians. Scholars tell us about his times and about the values of his contemporaries. Sometimes, researchers conclude that he didn't ever say some of the words attributed to him. Others have suggested that he never lived.

Whether or not the Gospels cite Jesus correctly, the Jesus of the Bible is the only Jesus that matters. His thoughts are internally consistent; they reflect a single philosophy. Oddly, there is one thing that scholars and academics have never done: they have never evaluated this philosophy. In other words, Western thinkers, for two millennia, have never taken Jesus seriously. They may have worshipped him, rejected him, or dispassionately studied his life and times. Yet they have never confronted his philosophy as philosophy. There has never been a critical reading of what he said. Surely Jesus is important enough to merit such an evaluation. I propose to do so now.

A central element in Christian thinking, based on the words of Jesus, is the doctrine of justification through faith. For Catholics, salvation can be achieved through faith and works; for Protestants, through faith alone. There is no Christian doctrine of salvation exclusively through works. Jesus spoke of faith in unambiguous terms:

> I am the resurrection, and the life: he that believeth in me, though he were dead, yet shall he live: and whosoever liveth and believeth in me shall never die. Believest thou this? (John 11:25-26)

Eternal life is the reward for faith. But what about those who have no faith? If we read carefully, we see that there is no hope for them:

> For God so loved the world, that he gave his only begotten Son, that whosoever believeth in him should not perish, but have everlasting life. For God sent not his Son into the world to condemn the world;

> but that the world through him might be saved. He that believeth in
> him is not condemned: but he that believeth not is condemned al-
> ready, because he hath not believed in the name of the only begotten
> Son of God. (John 3:16-18)

Faith, by definition, is different from knowledge. If we have knowledge, we
do not need faith. Faith involves believing what we do not know and perhaps
cannot know. It cannot be proved to a person who has experienced neither
heaven nor hell that these places exist, nor can it be conclusively demonstrated
to one still alive that a particular route is the only path to salvation. Jesus's miracles could show those who witnessed them that he multiplied loaves and fishes;
the miracles could not prove that he could grant life everlasting, although they
could create faith. George Bernard Shaw, in fact, defined a miracle as an event
that creates faith. This definition shows that Shaw considered faith something of
a miracle in its own right.

What happens to those who have no faith? Let us consider what Jesus said
about a certain rich man:

> There was a certain rich man, which was clothed in purple and fine
> linen, and fared sumptuously every day: and there was a certain beg-
> gar named Lazarus, which was laid at his gate, full of sores, and
> desiring to be fed with the crumbs which fell from the rich man's ta-
> ble: moreover the dogs came and licked his sores. And it came to
> pass, that the beggar died, and was carried by the angels into Abra-
> ham's bosom: the rich man also died, and was buried; and in hell he
> lifted up his eyes, being in torments, and seeth Abraham afar off, and
> Lazarus in his bosom. And he cried and said, Father Abraham, have
> mercy on me, and send Lazarus, that he may dip the tip of his finger
> in water, and cool my tongue; for I am tormented in this flame. But
> Abraham said, Son, remember that thou in thy lifetime receivedst thy
> good things, and likewise Lazarus evil things: but now he is com-
> forted, and thou art tormented. And beside all this, between us and
> you there is a great gulf fixed: so that they which would pass from
> hence to you cannot; neither can they pass to us, that would come
> from thence. Then he said, I pray thee therefore, father, that thou
> wouldest send him to my father's house: for I have five brethren; that
> he may testify unto them, lest they also come into this place of tor-
> ment. Abraham saith unto him, They have Moses and the prophets;
> let them hear them. And he said, Nay, father Abraham: but if one
> went unto them from the dead, they will repent. And he said unto
> him, If they hear not Moses and the prophets, neither will they be
> persuaded, though one rose from the dead. (Luke 16:19-31)

An ugly story. It tells us about the horror of eternal damnation. If the average contemporary reader does not experience this horror, it is no doubt because
we do not really believe in hell. In other words, we have no faith. The rich man
seems to be punished for selfishness and not for lack of faith, but if we look at
the words of the story, we see that it is indeed lack of faith that led him to his
fate: he is punished for not heeding Moses and the prophets, for lack of obedience to something he could not know about directly.

His brothers too will be asked to have faith; they will not be given the chance to talk to someone who has been to hell and can tell them what it is like. The argument offered by Abraham that they would not be persuaded by an eyewitness account is unconvincing. If people had a chance to question someone who had been there, or if they could see it themselves, they would not need faith; they would make a totally rational and informed decision. The rich man shows by his plea to save his brothers that his life would have been different had he simply had more direct knowledge. His wish to help them is entirely disinterested. Neither Abraham, a character within the account, nor Jesus, the narrator, recognizes this evidence of goodness. There is no forgiveness and no mercy for those in hell.

Good works are described by Jesus not as worthy in their own right but as deeds done to Jesus himself:

> When the Son of man shall come into his glory, and all the holy angels with him, then shall he sit upon the throne of his glory: and before him shall be gathered all nations: and he shall separate them one from another, as a shepherd divideth his sheep from the goats: and he shall set the sheep on his right hand, but the goats on the left. Then shall the King say unto them on his right hand, Come, ye blessed of my Father, inherit the kingdom prepared for you from the foundation of the world: for I was ahungered, and ye gave me meat: I was thirsty, and ye gave me drink: I was a stranger, and ye took me in: naked, and ye clothed me: I was sick, and ye visited me: I was in prison, and ye came unto me, Then shall the righteous answer him saying, Lord, when saw we thee ahungered, and fed thee? or thirsty, and gave thee drink? When saw we thee a stranger, and took thee in? or naked, and clothed thee? Or when saw we thee sick, or in prison, and came unto thee? And the King shall answer and say unto them, Verily I say unto you, Inasmuch as ye have done it unto one of the least of these my brethren, ye have done it to me. Then shall he also say unto them on the left hand, Depart from me, ye cursed, into everlasting fire, prepared for the devil and his angels: for I was ahungered, and ye gave me no meat: I was thirsty, and ye gave me no drink: I was a stranger, and ye took me not in: naked, and ye clothed me not: sick, and in prison, and ye visited me not. Then shall they also answer him, saying, Lord, when saw we thee ahungered, or athirst, or a stranger, or naked, or sick, or in prison, and did not minister unto thee? then shall he answer them, saying, Verily I say unto you, Inasmuch as ye did it not to one of the least of these, ye did it not to me. And these shall go away into everlasting punishment: but the righteous into life eternal. (Matthew 25:31-46)

It is beautiful to say that by serving others we serve God, but in a certain sense this minimizes the service. God needs us less than our fellow creatures do. Moreover, a deed done for its own sake is truly a good act; one done to gain reward or avoid punishment is merely a transaction. Faith in the reality of damnation may persuade us to be good because it pays to be, but somehow that is not really being good.

What about the poor goats? Like the rich man, they did not know what they were in for. They lacked the greatness of soul to want to feed the hungry and clothe the naked. They also lacked the faith that would have taught them they had better shape up or else. Only faith could have shown this to them. The knowledge that would have made goodness an act of enlightened self-interest was not available to them, as it is not available to anyone. They are still burning in hell. Then how can we say that "God sent not his Son into the world to condemn the world; but that the world through him might be saved"? The goats and the rich man were not given a fair chance.

The goats and the rich man—however disproportionate their punishment—were objectively lacking in mercy. There is a rough justice to their fates. Many of the parables, however, are stories where the point seems to be that there is no justice:

> For the kingdom of heaven is like unto a man that is a householder, which went out early in the morning to hire laborers into his vineyard. And when he had agreed with the laborers for a penny a day, he sent them into his vineyard. And he went out about the third hour, and saw others standing idle in the market place, and said unto them; Go ye also into the vineyard, and whatsoever is right I will give you. Again he went out about the sixth and ninth hour, and did likewise. And about the eleventh hour he went out, and found others standing idle, and saith unto them, Why stand ye here all the day idle? They say unto him, Because no man hath hired us. He saith unto them, Go ye also into the vineyard; and whatever is right, that shall ye receive. So when even was come, the lord of the vineyard saith unto his steward, Call the laborers, and give them their hire, beginning from the last unto the first. And when they came that were hired about the eleventh hour, they received every man a penny. But when the first came, they supposed that they should have received more; and they likewise received every man a penny. And when they had received it, they murmured against the goodman of the house, saying, These last have wrought but one hour, and thou hast made them equal unto us, which have borne the burden and heat of the day. But he answered one of them, and said, Friend, I do thee no wrong: didst not thou agree with me for a penny? Take that thine is and go thy way: I will give unto this last, even as unto thee. Is it not lawful for me to do what I will wish with mine own? Is thine eye evil, because I am good? So the last shall be first, and the first last: for many be called, but few chosen. (Matthew 20:1-16)

Is this parable meant to teach anything? Is it simply recognition of the fact that life is unfair? But it is not about life; it begins with the words, "For the kingdom of heaven is like. . . ." Whatever its meaning, it reminds us of a different instance of injustice:

> Now it came to pass, as they went, that he encountered into a certain village: and a certain woman named Martha received him into her house. And she had a sister called Mary, which sat at Jesus' feet, and heard his word. But Martha was cumbered about much serving, and

came to him, and said, Lord, dost thou not care that my sister hath
left me to serve alone? bid her therefore that she help me. And Jesus
answered and said unto her, Martha, Martha, thou art careful and
troubled about many things: but one thing is needful: and Mary hath
chosen that good part, which shall not be taken away from her.
(Luke 10:38-42)

The answer of a male chauvinist, who takes it for granted that women serve
him. Martha too would have preferred to sit at Jesus' feet. Yet the openness of
Jesus with women has been cited as an example of his respect for women's
rights in a patriarchal age. So has his disapproval of divorce, which at the time
and place he lived was a unilateral act by the man. But if we look at Jesus'
words, his condemnation of divorce seems to have nothing to do with women's
rights:

It hath been said, Whosoever shall put away his wife, let him give her
a writing of divorcement: But I say unto you, That whosoever put
away his wife, saving for the cause of fornication, causeth her to
commit adultery: and whosoever shall marry her that is divorced
committeth adultery. (Matthew 5:31-32)

There is no hint or tone suggesting a concern for women's position in this
passage. What we see instead is the view that marrying a divorced woman (there
is no mention of a divorced man) is adultery. The gravity of this sin in shown in
the verses that immediately precede this citation:

Ye have heard that it was said by them of old time, Thou shalt not
commit adultery: but I say unto you, That whosoever looketh on a
woman to lust after her hath committed adultery already with her in
his heart. And if thy right eye offend thee, pluck it out, and cast it
from thee: for it is profitable for thee that one of thy members should
perish, and not that thy whole body should be cast into hell.
(Matthew 5:27-29)

Wow! It is better to be blind than to look at a woman with lust. And what if
a woman looks at a man with lust? The possibility is not mentioned. It is reasonable to conclude, however, that these passages are not concerned with anything
so mundane as women's rights. They are a rejection of sexual desire—not adultery, just simple looking with lust, something that everybody does every day.
These are perhaps the most anti-sexual words ever written.

The assertion that thinking, or at least lusting, is as bad as *doing* leads us
back to the question of faith. Desire can be controlled, but short of plucking out
one's eye, it cannot be eliminated. It is simply there, like faith or lack of faith.
And like lack of faith, it is a reason to burn in hell. This makes no sense. Why
should honest doubt, or honest desire for that matter, be a punishable offense? It
only makes sense if the purpose of life is to have faith. We are told this directly.
Salvation comes through faith in Jesus:

Jesus saith unto him, I am the way, the truth, and the life: no man
cometh unto the Father, but by me. (John 14:6)

The Inquisition followed as the night the day.

The New Testament offers a consistent view throughout. The purpose of life is to achieve salvation, which is done partly (for Catholics) or entirely (for Protestants) by accepting Jesus' sacrifice through our faith in him. Obligations to the living and the dead do not count unless, as in the cases of the rich man and the goats, these duties are redefined as obligations to Jesus:

> And another of his disciples said unto him, Lord, suffer me first to go and bury my father. But Jesus said unto him, Follow me; and let the dead bury their dead. (Matthew 8:21-22)

It was Jesus' insistence that service to him was more important than concern about sentiment and society that enraged Judas and led him to betray Jesus:

> Now when Jesus was in Bethany, in the house of Simon the leper, there came unto him a woman having an alabaster box of very precious ointment, and poured it on his head, as he sat at meat. But when his disciples saw it, they had indignation, saying, To what purpose is this waste? For this ointment might have been sold for much, and given to the poor. When Jesus understood it, he said unto them, Why trouble ye the woman? for she hath wrought a good work upon me. For ye have the poor always with you; but me ye have not always. For in that she had poured this ointment on my body, she did it for my burial. Verily I say unto you, Wheresoever this gospel shall be preached in the whole world, there shall also this, that this woman hath done, be told for a memorial of her. Then one of the twelve, called Judas Iscariot, went unto the chief priests, and said unto them, What will ye give me, and I will deliver him unto you? And they covenanted with him for thirty pieces of silver. (Matthew 26:6-15)

The account by Matthew does not make any connection between Jesus' words and Judas' motivation for his act of betrayal. Money is not the issue, because Judas agrees to deliver Jesus before he knows what the reward will be. John, who does make the connection, maintains that Judas simply wanted to steal the money destined for the poor:

> Then Jesus six days before the passover came to Bethany, where Lazarus was which had been dead, whom he raised from the dead. There they made him a supper; and Martha served: but Lazarus was one of them that sat at the table with him. Then took Mary a pound of ointment of spikenard, very costly, and anointed the feet of Jesus, and wiped his feet with her hair: and the house was filled with the odor of ointment. Then saith one of the disciples, Judas Iscariot, Simon's son, which should betray him, Why was not this ointment sold for three hundred pence, and given to the poor? This he said, not that he cared for the poor; but because he was a thief, and had the bag, and bare what was put therein. Then said Jesus, Let her alone: against the day of my burying hath she kept this. For the poor always ye have with you; but me ye have not always. (John 12:1-8)

Matthew, who does not question the reasons for the disciples' indignation, does not mention Judas. As long as Judas is not referred to directly, the indignation seems logical. John cannot allow Judas to appear more concerned for the poor than Jesus is, so he must invent another motive for Judas' objection. When we read the Matthew and John accounts together, we see that the disciple who was offended by Jesus' words was Judas, who then went out to betray Jesus before he knew what his monetary reward would be.

Jesus knew that the reason for his sojourn on earth was to be crucified so that he himself could bear the punishment for the sins of humanity:

> Then he opened their understanding, that they might understand the Scriptures, and said unto them, Thus is it written, and thus it behooved Christ to suffer, and to rise from the dead the third day: and that repentance and remission of sins should be preached among all nations, beginning at Jerusalem. (Luke 24:45-47)

It follows that his submission to suffering on the cross was a voluntary act—indeed a necessary one. Jesus unambiguously contradicts Pilate's claim to have the power of life and death over Jesus:

> Then Pilate said unto him, Speakest thou not unto me? knowest thou not that I have the power to crucify thee, and have the power to release thee? Jesus answered, Thou couldest have no power at all against me, except it were given thee from above: therefore he that delivered me unto thee hath the greater sin. (John 19:10-11)

This is hard to understand. "He that delivered me unto thee" is no doubt Judas, who was also given his power to do so from above. Why is this a reason for Judas' sin to be greater than Pilate's? We have already been told that Judas was selected to be a disciple precisely because he was needed to perform the duty of the betrayal that would lead to Jesus' suffering and the consequent redemption of the world:

> Jesus answered them, Have I not chosen you twelve, and one of you is a devil? He spake of Judas Iscariot the son of Simon: for he it was that should betray him, being one of the twelve. (John 6:70-71)

The cross is a symbol revered by Christians because Jesus' agony was the means to salvation—the central miracle of Christianity. Then why should not Judas be equally honored? Had there been no betrayal, there would have been no road to salvation. In fact, the recently translated *Gospel of Judas,* probably written in Greek in approximately 180 C.E. and later translated into Coptic, cites Jesus as telling Judas that he is the most beloved of the disciples.

Despite the internal coherence of the New Testament, many questions remain unanswered. If God wished to save humanity from the horrible consequences of sin, why did this have to be done through suffering? Apparently the punishment has to go someplace. God cannot simply forgive the sin; a scapegoat is needed. Jesus' sacrifice then is a noble and beautiful act; God himself is the scapegoat. But why must there be punishment? For negative reinforcement? Then the rules and penalties should be made well known. For justice? Then the idea of a scapegoat is abhorrent.

Forgiveness needs no excuse and no explanation. Diversion of the punishment to Jesus is not the same as forgiveness, since by its nature it negates the ideas of both mercy and justice. Besides, God cannot be punished. If Jesus is entirely man, he is nevertheless entirely God. Jesus the man can suffer, but since he is simultaneously divine, his suffering, however real, cannot hurt him. Jesus the man can die and be resurrected, but God is eternal, so his death is inconsequential and his resurrection entirely natural.

For those Christians who have faith in the justice and mercy of God, these questions do not exist. Yet even during the Age of Faith there were those who did not believe. Not only were they damned if we accept Jesus' teaching; their ideas could lead others to damnation. The beliefs of the faithful had to be protected. Those who sentenced freethinkers and heretics to burn at the stake were not necessarily cruel people; they were simply following the logic of the doctrine of justification through faith.

Nowadays, Christian clergy and Christian laity, with few exceptions, believe in freedom of religion. Without directly confronting the issue, they have abandoned the doctrine of justification through faith.

Chapter 9

Reconsidering Abraham

Did God whimsically decide to test Abraham by commanding him to sacrifice his son Isaac and then, at the last minute, tell him he didn't have to? Does the story have a happy ending, since Abraham passed the test and a few days of anxiety don't matter, since all's well that ends well? The story of the binding of Isaac, told in Chapter 22 of the Book of Genesis, may be read from either a historical or a religious point of view. The text itself, if we are willing to accept it as true, leaves all sorts of questions unanswered, essentially because these questions are never asked: Was Abraham Isaac's biological father or did Abimelech, King of Gerar, sire Isaac? Since Sarah was Abraham's half-sister, can it be that Abraham and Sarah never had sexual relations with each other? Since God commanded Abraham to sacrifice his son directly, but commanded him not to do so indirectly, through an angel, can it be that Abraham invented or imagined the angel? And if that's what Abraham did, did he feel he didn't have to go through with the sacrifice since Isaac was only his adopted son?

Let us examine the historical interpretation first. Although there is no evidence, other than the Book of Genesis itself, that Abraham or Isaac existed, the story may be read as a document concerned with end of the practice of sacrificing one's first-born son. We know from various other parts of the Bible that child sacrifice was practiced by various nations in Biblical times: "And the Avites made Nibhaz and Tartak, and the Sepharvites burnt their children in the fire to Adrammelech and Anammelech, the gods of the Sepharvaim" (2 Kings 17:31). We are even presented with one account where child sacrifice actually works:

> And when the king of Moab saw that the battle was too sore for him, he took with him seven hundred men that drew swords, to break through even unto the king of Edom: but they could not. Then he took his eldest son that should have reigned in his stead, and offered him for a burnt offering upon the wall. And there was great indignation against Israel: and they departed from him, and returned to their own land. (2 Kings 3:26-27)

Abraham was clearly not the only father who ever felt called upon to offer his child as a sacrifice. Indeed, the practice apparently had been adopted in Jeremiah's time even in the land of Judah, and Jeremiah denounced it: "And they [the children of Judah] have built the high places of Tophet, which is in the valley of the son of Hinnom, to burn their sons and their daughters in the fire; which I commanded them not, neither came it into my heart" (Jer. 7:31). The Hebrew word for "hell," *gehinnom*, means "valley of Hinnom," in other words, "valley of child sacrifice."

To this day, the Jewish custom of *Pidyon Ha-ben*, where one pays a *kohen*, a descendant of the ancient priestly caste, to redeem a first-born son, shows the discomfort that Jews must have felt at one time about not performing this sacrifice. In the Book of Numbers we read, "Every thing that openeth the matrix [womb] in all flesh, which they bring unto the Lord, whether it be of men or beasts, shall be thine: nevertheless the first-born of man shalt thou surely redeem, and the firstling of unclean beasts shalt thou redeem" (18:15).

Archeological evidence exists to support the biblical charges that child sacrifice was practiced among neighboring peoples. The Carthaginians, descended from the Phoenicians, did so, according to an article in the September 1, 1987, issue of *The New York Times*. Under the headline, "Relics of Carthage Show Brutality Amid the Good Life," we read the following: "A trove of relics now arriving in New York contains evidence that the ritual slaying of children in ancient Carthage was so common that it helped control the growth of the population and helped families keep fortunes intact over generations, archeologists say."

As late as the time of the New Testament, the idea of the efficacy of child sacrifice survives; God sacrifices his only begotten son to spare mankind from the consequences of sin by diverting the punishment to himself—in other words, as a sin offering.

Abraham is called the first Jew. Why not Jacob, renamed Israel, the father of the 12 tribes? Why not Moses, who received the Torah—the law that defines Jews? Abraham's very name suggests that he is no more linked to the Jewish people than to several other nations; in Genesis 17 we are told it means *av hamon goyim* (father of many nations).

Why Abraham? One answer has to be that the abandonment of child sacrifice was a defining moment in the history of the creation of Judaism. A second reason is that Abraham is linked in Jewish tradition to the end of idolatry. Abraham was an iconoclast, an idol breaker. In the Aggadah (rabbinical narrations, not to be regarded as authoritative, that form part of the literature of the Oral Law), Abraham's father, Terah, made and sold idols (Breshit Rabbah 38:12). He once left Abraham in charge of his business, and when he returned, all the idols were smashed except for the largest. Abraham explained that the idols had gotten into an argument over a sacrifice, and that the biggest idol had won the fight. This is the same Abraham who did not sacrifice his son Isaac.

Was Abraham showing obedience to God when he bound Isaac and placed him on the altar? Certainly, if we read the text exactly as it was written. But no more so than when other fathers did the same thing. The importance of the story is that Abraham did *not* sacrifice Isaac. If we are to respect Abraham, it must be because he was an innovator. This remains true whether we believe there was a historical Abraham or whether we look upon the story of the binding of Isaac as an allegory.

Abraham's willingness to obey God even to the point of sacrificing his son is traditionally taken as evidence of his goodness and moral strength, since he puts God's commandment above his own emotions. Abraham's compliance implies that obedience to the Lord takes priority over such commandments as "Thou shalt not kill." To be sure, the Ten Commandments had not yet been given to Moses, who was not to be born for several generations. But from a historical point of view, the story may be read in a different way, as an example of Abraham's originality and courage. His contribution was the beginning of a new religion that both ended idolatry and prohibited all forms of human sacrifice. Otherwise, his willingness to obey the command to offer his son would simply be an example both of lack of originality and of callousness.

Let us now consider the binding of Isaac from a religious point of view. Abraham had been quite callous when Sarah asked him to drive his son Ishmael and Ishmael's mother, Hagar, into the desert. But God told him it would be all right: "Let it not be grievous in thy sight because of the lad, and because of thy bondwoman; in all that Sarah hath said unto thee, hearken unto her voice; for in Isaac shall thy seed be called" (Gen. 21:12). Abraham did not point out that driving people into the wilderness was heartless. He didn't have to look at Hagar and Ishmael suffering from thirst in the desert; all the same, he knew what deserts were like. Let us examine a detail from this story: "And the water was spent in the bottle, and she cast the child under one of the shrubs. And she went, and sat down over against him a good way off, as it were a bowshot: for she said, Let me not see the death of the child. And she sat over against him, and lift up her voice and wept" (Gen. 21:15-16).

It is possible to say that Abraham's trust in God was not misplaced; both Ishmael and Isaac were rescued in the nick of time. Then we are left with the fact of Abraham's silence. This very silence could be considered further evidence of Abraham's virtue, since it is an example of unquestioning faith. But we know that God did not demand silence from Abraham, as is shown by the story of Abraham's argument with God over the destruction of Sodom and Gomorrah. If God did not require silence, then Abraham's reluctance to argue in the face of imminent death becomes criminal. If God did not require silence, then Abraham's faith is nothing more than the abandonment of morality and thought, and his binding of Isaac is both unthinking and timid.

But perhaps God did indeed demand silence. Let us look at Genesis 22:2, where God said, "Take now thy son, thine only son Isaac, whom thou lovest, and get thee unto the land of Moriah; and offer him there for a burnt offering upon one of the mountains which I will tell thee of." By saying "thine only son Isaac, whom thou lovest," God was telling Abraham not to argue, since he already knew Abraham's argument. He knew that Ishmael was no longer a functioning son, since he had been driven away, and for all Abraham knew,

Ishmael might not even be alive. God's words to Abraham were a commandment, whereas in the case of Sodom and Gomorrah, God had merely informed
Abraham of his plans, leaving Abraham free to argue. The whole idea of sacrificing one's first-born son was that it gave to God someone who was not only
loved but who represented one's future and one's hopes. In the face of such a
commandment, Abraham had no choice but to be timid.

The commandment came from God. The counter-order came from an angel:
"And the angel of the Lord called unto him out of heaven, and said, Abraham,
Abraham; and he said Here am I. And he said, Lay not thine hand upon the lad,
neither do thou anything unto him: for now I know that thou fearest God, seeing
thou hast not withheld thy son, thine only son from me" (Gen. 22:11-12). It is
extremely odd that God's voice spoke directly to Abraham when telling him to
perform the sacrifice but indirectly via an angel when telling him not to hurt
Isaac. Every detail of the Bible is supposed to be significant. What is the signifi-
cance of the third-person pardon Abraham received? Perhaps God wasn't sure
he wanted to release Abraham from his obligation to sacrifice Isaac. Perhaps
Abraham, alone on the mountain, imagined the angel or made him up and reported the story when he came down from the mountain. The text does not tell
us that this happened, but the very fact that God did not speak to Abraham directly at this critical moment, when a direct reward or at least a direct
compliment was in order, should set us thinking. Furthermore, God never spoke
to Abraham again.

Rashi, Rabbi Solomon ben Isaac, who lived from 1040 to 1105, is considered by many to be the first and greatest commentator on the Hebrew Bible. In
his comments on Genesis 25:19, he tries to refute the idea that Isaac was not
Abraham's son at all but rather the son of Abimelech, king of Gerar, a Philistine
city. Rashi's attempt at refutation leads us back to the text of Genesis in order to
see why Rashi felt that it needed to be done in the first place.

In Genesis 20:2 we are told, "And Abraham said of Sarah his wife, she is
my sister: and Abimelech king of Gerar sent, and took Sarah." God came to
Abimelech in a dream and told him that Sarah was Abraham's wife. "Then
Abimelech called Abraham, and said unto him, What hast thou done unto us?
and what have I offended thee, that thou hast brought on me and my kingdom a
great sin? thou hast done deeds unto me that ought not to be done" (Gen. 20: 9).
We were told in verse 4 that Abimelech had not touched Sarah, but his words to
Abraham sound as if he had indeed transgressed with Sarah. Abraham explains
his omission as a result of his fear: "Surely the fear of God is not in this place;
and they will slay me for my wife's sake. And yet indeed she is my sister; she is
the daughter of my father, but not the daughter of my mother; and she became
my wife" (Gen. 20:11-12).

Abimelech then gave many gifts to Abraham. "And unto Sarah he said, Behold, I have given thy brother a thousand pieces of silver: behold, he is to thee a
covering of the eyes, unto all that are with thee, and with all other: thus she was
reproved" (20:16). The meaning of the verse is unclear, but the size of the gift
does suggest that Abimelech, albeit unknowingly, had committed adultery with
Sarah and was trying to atone for his sin. And in the next two verses, we see that

Abimelech and his people were punished until Abraham prayed for them: "So Abraham prayed unto God: and God healed Abimelech, and his wife, and their maidservants; and they bare children. For the Lord had fast closed up all the wombs of the house of Abimelech, because of Sarah, Abraham's wife" (20:17-18). We then go directly to Chapter 21, which begins with the words "And the Lord visited Sarah as he had said, and the Lord did unto Sarah as he had spoken. For Sarah conceived, and bare Abraham a son in his old age, at the set time of which God had spoken to him" (21:1-2). The phrase "bare Abraham a son" does not say that Sarah bore Abraham his own biological son.

Except for the denial in verse 4, which can be explained as an attempt by Abimelech to protect himself, the rest of Chapter 20 is clearly telling us that Abimelech had sexual relations with Sarah and was punished for it. Sarah then becomes pregnant. No wonder Rashi had to try to prove that Isaac was Abraham's son. He goes about it by referring to Genesis 25:19, where there is a repetition of Isaac's ancestry. Rashi tells us, "Since the verse wrote 'Isaac son of Abraham,' it had to say 'Abraham begot Isaac' for the scoffers of the generation were saying 'Sarah became pregnant from Abimelech.' For she had spent many years with Abraham as his wife, yet she did not become pregnant from him. What did the Holy One, Blessed is He, do? He fashioned the form of Isaac's face to resemble Abraham's, and everyone attested Abraham begot Isaac."

Rashi's explanation is not convincing. If Isaac had resembled Abraham from the time he was born, the scoffers Rashi is referring to wouldn't have scoffed. It was only as a result of the scoffing that God changed Isaac's face to look like Abraham's. Unlike the story cited above of Abraham's breaking the idols in his father's shop, which links the end of idolatry to the end of child sacrifice by telling us that Abraham rejected both these practices, Rashi's story contradicts the most likely meaning of the text of Genesis 20. Rashi understood that Genesis points to Abimelech as Isaac's father, so he had to invent a story to contradict the text.

Isaac's name in Hebrew is Yitzhak, which is a form of the verb meaning 'to laugh' and refers to Sarah's laughter when she heard she would bear a son, since she was "after the manner of women" (18:11), or post-menopausal. When we read Chapter 18, we do not yet know Sarah is Abraham's half-sister, even though Abraham had told that story to Pharaoh in Chapter 12, when it appeared to be a simple lie. Continuing in Genesis, past the story of Abimelech, another possibility presents itself: Perhaps Sarah hadn't become pregnant, perhaps she laughed at the prediction she would have a child, because she was a virgin. She and her half-brother were married, to be sure, but they perhaps they couldn't bring themselves to consummate their marriage because they were siblings. We are never told this, but it is a possibility. On the other hand, we are told in Chapter 20 that despite Abimelech's claim that he did not have sex relations with Sarah, he was punished for having done so.

Both Rashi and the rabbis who wrote the Aggadah composed or collected stories to support or deny meanings implicit or explicit in Biblical texts. None of them, to my knowledge, suggested that the reason Abraham claimed or imagined he heard an angel telling him not to sacrifice Isaac was that he felt he could get away with it. When God told him to sacrifice his son, his only son, whom he loved, maybe he thought to himself that Isaac was not his biological son but Abimelech's. When God commanded Abraham to sacrifice the person he loved most, the person who was his hope for the future of a nation that would not worship idols, he had an out. The sacrifice demanded of him wasn't quite so great as it sounded. He differed from all the other fathers of his time and place who sacrificed their biological children. Abraham's biological son, Ishmael, was lost, and his beloved heir was adopted. If a sacrifice isn't total, he might have thought, one doesn't have to do it.

If God knew all the time that he would release Abraham from his duty to sacrifice Isaac, then the story of the binding is merely a test—a type of practical joke. But since the Bible introduces the possibility that Abraham may not have been Isaac's biological father, a literal reading of the text introduces a great many more problems than a historical interpretation. Abraham, the historical figure, or the allegorical figure referring to a real moment in history, was the first person to understand that idols were only sculptures. He dared to understand that human sacrifice has always been wrong. The Biblical story, with its introduction of the doubt about Isaac's paternity, cannot be understood. The historical or allegorical Abraham, on the other hand, is one of the heroes of history. He introduced the traditions of arguing and questioning into religion. That is why he is the first Jew.

Chapter 10

Reconsidering 20th Century Music

A few years ago, my wife and I subscribed to a chamber music series. No matter who was performing, the program followed the same canonical form: a quartet by Haydn, a modern work, the intermission, and a concluding piece from the romantic period. If the performers were not a string quartet but some other chamber group—for example, a quintet or an ensemble including a wind instrument—the first work on the program was by Mozart rather than Haydn, a sensible choice: Haydn's string quartets are better than Mozart's, but Mozart's other chamber pieces are better than Haydn's. What is significant, however, is the fact that whoever planned these concerts knew that the contemporary composition had to be in the middle. If the 20th-century piece came first, the audience would arrive late; if it concluded the concert, the audience would walk out after the intermission.

We did not renew our subscription. A modern piece is the price you pay for going to a concert, and I am not willing to pay the price.

The schedulers were behaving rationally. They wanted to help modern composers and at the same time educate the audience. We all know that the music of the last century has not won a big audience. In the words of Kingsley Amis, quoted in Paul Fussell's *The Anti-Egotist*, "Twentieth-century music is like paedophilia. No matter how persuasively and persistently its champions urge their cause, it will never be accepted by the public at large, who will continue to regard it with incomprehension, outrage and repugnance" (p. 129).

Has there ever before been a period in which audiences specifically rejected the music of their own contemporaries? Probably not. In the late 19th century, however, music split into classical and popular. Classical music was directed to an ever narrower public. Perhaps that is why our own age is the only recorded period when we scorn the creations of our contemporaries. Our music is not designed to be liked at first hearing. We have to be maneuvered into listening to it by those who schedule concerts.

Paul Fussell, cited above, suggests a possible reason for this state of affairs in his discussion of Kingsley Amis's opposition to modernism. He says that "there is built into Modernism a hatred—and that is not too strong a word—of ordinary people . . . (p. 67)." There was, however, a form of contemporary music that Kingsley Amis did not consider modernist: jazz. "Jazz was the music that mattered, not only contemporary, happening all the time, but immediately attractive, no sooner heard than delightedly responded to" (p. 128). Nevertheless, Amis changed his mind. He began to dislike jazz when it became intellectually respectable—when "it began to be studied in universities." At that point, jazz was taken away from the people; it became a tool of the enemy, the elite.

Jazz is 20th-century music. It developed together with other forms of contemporary music. What happened is that with time it became less and less bound by the principle of tonality.

The greatest music the world has ever known is tonal. No one has successfully defined greatness, but whatever it is, it is recognizable. All societies and all times have had music, and all have produced geniuses. But there is one particular music that arose in a particular place—Germany and Italy—and at a particular time—the 17th century. It lasted 300 years and completed its life span. It is the world's music. There is nothing else like it. It is comparable to ancient Greek drama, another privileged moment in history. This magic, wonderful music is the realization of a phenomenon known as tonality. A piece is in a particular key, and the melodies and harmonies of the music lead us to the tonic, the first note of the scale of the key in which the piece is written, the note which gives us the feeling that the musical phrase has reached its conclusion: the triad whose lowest note is the tonic note that necessarily is the last chord in the composition. In other words, the composition is going somewhere. We don't know what the route will be if we are unfamiliar with the piece, but the destination is—pre-destined.

Harmony and tonality are physical realities. Music is a series of pitches and combinations of pitches played in rhythmic patterns. Pitch is the way we hear frequency, the number of vibrations per second produced by a voice or a musical instrument. If we hear an A and a C-sharp at the same time, the combination sounds harmonious. We call the distance between these notes the interval of a third, in this case, a major third. When two notes are a major third from each other, the ratio of the vibrations is 4 to 5. The A string vibrates at 440 cycles per second and the C-sharp string at 550. C-sharp and E form a minor third, which also sounds harmonious. The ratio of vibrations is 5 to 6, E having a pitch of 660. A minor third on top of a major third is called a major triad, one of the basic chords of Western music. The interval between the outer notes of the triad is called a fifth, and the ratio of the pitches is necessarily 2 to 3. In the case of a major triad formed by A, C-sharp and E, the outer notes, with pitches of 440 and 660, illustrate the 2 to 3 ratio.

Major and minor thirds, so typical of Western music, occurred in the music of the late Middle Ages and the Renaissance, and madrigals of the 16th century were likely to end on a tonic chord. There is no clear answer to the question of when the incidental harmonies that occurred in the polyphonic music of the 16th century, where each voice sang its own line, turned into the harmonic music of the 17th and 18th centuries, where the different musical lines were all moving together as melodies heading toward a conclusion: a tonic chord preceded by a dominant chord, the chord built on the fifth note of the scale. We have seen above that the first and fifth notes of the scale have pitches with vibrations per second in the ratio of 2 to 3. The sequence of a triad on the fifth note of a scale followed by one on the first note, for some unknown reason, produces a feeling of finality.

The ratio of pitches is a physical fact; the reason this ratio is satisfying cannot be explained. "Tonal motion is therefore always directed: it is always felt as motion toward or away from some state of tension or relaxation," says Neil M. Ribe, writing in the November 1987 issue of *Commentary* ("Atonal Music and Its Limits"). Atonal music, according to Ribe, replaces common sense with mathematical abstractions. Somehow, Ribe hasn't explained why atonality is hard to like. After all, a ratio of 2 to 3 is also a mathematical abstraction. Knowing the physics of tonality hasn't helped us. We know tonality is real but we do not know why a particular ratio of vibrations in a particular sequence should produce a pleasing effect.

Arnold Schoenberg invented serial music, in which all twelve notes of the chromatic scale were used and none could be repeated until all had been played. He called it "emancipation of the dissonance" (see Ribe), but the dissonance could not be emancipated. The human brain accepts certain sequences as beautiful and rejects others as ugly. Schoenberg's mistake was his belief that harmony and tonality are cultural constructs. They aren't. The whole world prefers tonality.

Perhaps we can link the increased use of tonality and the consequent rise of Western music as we know it with the first opera, Jacopo Peri's *Euridice*, which premiered on February 9, 1600. A plot, according to Aristotle, should have a beginning, a middle, and an end. When music was linked to story, the music too needed a sense of direction, which tonality provided. It is interesting to note that the great plays of ancient Greece were performed to musical accompaniments that are lost. We love these plays, but they are incomplete without their music. Was the music that accompanied the plays of Sophocles tonal? Would the plays be more powerful if performed with this music? Would we admire the music today as we do the plays? We will never know.

Our own operas, unlike Greek drama, are loved primarily for their music. No one would care to see the silly plot of Schikaneder's *The Magic Flute* performed without Mozart's music. Richard Wagner, who revived the term "music drama," tried to create works where the importance of plot and music were equal. Yet even in the case of Wagner, we may enjoy listening to his music without seeing the opera, but we wouldn't choose to see dramas extolling the inherent beauty of stupidity, as Wagner's operas do, if they weren't accompanied by Wagner's music. If the development of music drama led to the increased use of tonality in music—and we cannot be sure that it did—the tonal music of the first 300 years of opera stands on its own, plot or no plot.

The 17th century was the childhood of Western music. It reached its adult-hood in the 18th century, with a group of composers all born in 1685: Domenico Scarlatti, George Frideric Handel, and Johann Sebastian Bach. In Bach, the most conservative of the three, polyphonic music reached its culmination. Neverthe-less, Bach could write compositions based on melody and harmony that belonged to his past and his future at the same time. The generation of 1685, and their contemporary, Antonio Vivaldi, changed the status of music, making it into something immortal, something loved and recognized everywhere. Scholars have analyzed the contrapuntal, harmonic and melodic structures of their works, but no one has ever understood its greatness.

Styles changed with Haydn and Mozart, but greatness remained. I remem-ber when I first saw Mozart's *The Marriage of Figaro*. It was in 1952 or 53, and I was fifteen. I heard the aria "Dove sono," and I was overwhelmed by the beauty of its melody. I went home and tried to play it on the piano. It was very simple: a turn, C—D C B C, followed by another turn a third higher: E—F E D E. Child's play. What makes it so wonderful? Genius remains a mystery.

Style continued to change. Beethoven extended the idea of tonality by using many changes of key in his development sections. His symphonies were longer and his orchestration thicker than anything his audience had ever heard. Yet people went to hear his compositions. When Beethoven's works were pre-miered, the entire concert generally consisted of contemporary pieces, often all premieres by the same composer. Were audiences more tolerant of the new in those days? What a silly question. Tolerance hadn't been invented yet. People were willing to listen to new compositions because music wasn't ugly then. Oc-casionally an innovative piece got a bad review, but a year or so later, the audience had learned to love it.

Beethoven never earned enough money from his compositions. Neverthe-less, we cannot conclude from this that he was unappreciated. His 9th Symphony, an innovative work, was received with great enthusiasm despite the fact that the composer netted only 420 florins from its premiere performance. At Beethoven's funeral, the crowds were enormous and soldiers had to be called to make way for the procession. We have all heard the story of how Mozart's body was unaccompanied to the grave, but according to *Mozart in Vienna*, a biogra-phy by Volkmar Braunbehrens, "accompanying the coffin to the gravesite was unusual at the time" (p. 419). Mozart's works were quite popular in his lifetime, and his opera *The Marriage of Figaro* was universally appreciated. In an era when most people were peasants and laborers, the rest of the population, the middle and upper classes, loved and admired serious music. It is hard to know how to compare the percentages of music lovers in different types of society, but we can be sure that Mozart and Beethoven were major cultural figures in a way that composers of classical music today can never be.

Wagner was perhaps the first composer who was really hard to get used to. His melodies were longer and often slower than what had come before. It was not always so clear where the melody was heading. Perhaps he was the first modernist. I will define a modernist creative artist as one who attempts to re-shape and even recreate his audience. Instead of saying, "Try it. You'll like it," as Beethoven might have, the modernist says, "You won't like this, but if you're good and work hard, you can become one of my admirers." Instead of saying, "Lend me your ears," the modernist says, "Give me your ears—and your soul. I will give you better ones."

Mahler's 6th Symphony is a composition dating from 1904. It barely made it into the 20th century. I have always liked and admired the music of Mahler, a gifted composer, but when he got to the last movement of what could have been a great symphony, he went overboard. He wrote a movement that was too long and too bombastic. It was filled with false conclusions, where the audience thinks the piece is over and breathes a sigh of relief, only to find that there is more to come.

Did something major and irrevocable happen in 1904, between the composition of the third and fourth movements of Mahler's 6th Symphony? I think so. Mahler set the stage for Arnold Schoenberg and atonal music. A century has passed, but it has never become popular. It is both outdated and too modern.

Klaus Tennstedt, a conductor famous for his interpretations of Mahler, died on January 11, 1998. His obituary in the New York Times, on January 13, quoted him as having said, "At least for traditional instruments, I believe that everything has already been composed." If that is the case, Schoenberg had no choice but to invent a new art form. As we know, it is called serial or atonal music, but a better name might have been anti-tonal music.

Tennstedt in effect recognized that the Western music that began in the 17th century had completed its life span. Perhaps Schoenberg agreed as well. He expected serial music to become popular. He never thought he was composing for academics only.

Kingsley Amis, as we saw above, hated modernism, which he identified with being studied in a university. Audiences hate modernism too. An audience owes a creator nothing. And nothing is what the creator generally receives. We all know stories about how Marcel Proust or James Joyce received multiple rejections. When Proust and Joyce became famous, the joke was on the publishers who had rejected them. But those who eventually get published are the exceptions. Most compositions are never performed; most books, never printed. It can happen that an unknown creative artist is recognized two or three centuries later; Antonio Vivaldi is an example. But usually, it doesn't happen, and the undiscovered artist remains undiscovered.

This is very sad. Nevertheless, the audience owes the creator nothing. Nobody should have to read through *Finnegan's Wake*, and indeed nobody does. T.S. Eliot's *The Waste Land*, with its (deliberately?) useless notes at the end, is a great work, but if we don't get very much past the wonderful first line, "April is the cruellest month," that is not our fault. If there is any fault at all, it is Eliot's. His poem sounds as if it was written in order to be studied at a university. Writers may choose to demand a great deal of attention and knowledge from readers, but readers need not give in to their demands.

20th-century composers do demand. By trying to reshape their listeners, they inevitably have an adversary relationship with their public. It is their privilege to bully their potential audience; they create as they feel they must. Similarly, it is the privilege of audiences to ignore and reject what they find ugly.

In the case of 20th-century politics, totalitarianism echoed the demands of art. Just as thought reform was an explicit goal of Communist regimes, so taste reform is an implicit goal of modernist creators.

Totalitarian rulers and philosophers attempt to control not only society but the human soul itself. Music, for whatever reason, delights the soul, just as literature delights the mind. Greek drama, with its accompanying music, was roughly contemporary with Athenian democracy. It fizzled out when Plato's *Republic* appeared, which introduced the concept of a noble lie, to be accepted by the rulers and the community in general: ". . . all of you in this land are brothers; but the god who fashioned you mixed gold in the composition of those among you who are fit to rule, so that they are of the most precious quality; and he put silver in the Auxiliaries, and iron and brass in the craftsmen" (Book III:414). Thought control with a vengeance!

Plato also would not have tolerated the manufacture of the flute or other instruments "capable of modulation into all the modes" (Book III: 398-400). He feared the enormous emotional power of music. Indeed, Ayatollah Khomeini, in his way an example of Plato's ideal of the Philosopher King, banned Western music from Iranian radio stations. During Chairman Mao's Great Proletarian Cultural Revolution, most music and theater were prohibited, except the eight revolutionary operas selected by Jiang Qing, Mao's wife.

The 20th century, the era that saw the rise and decline of totalitarianism, was an esthetic failure. What happened in music happened in the other arts as well. Music, art, poetry, novels, cities, roadsides—everywhere there are new forms of ugliness. Even the human body has been uglified. People are beautiful. Yet our current fashions are changing this. Piercing and tattooing are completing the work started by Mahler in 1904.

Architecture is the one art that has not succumbed to the uglification of our era. Architecture must fill a practical purpose; buildings must stand and be usable, which means that architects are not free to hate the public. That is why the Guggenheim Museum is a better work of art than the paintings displayed in it. But what is a better work of art? There is often a consensus on the answer, but a consensus is not the same thing as a criterion. We all judge art, all the time. Many of us, perhaps most of us, have felt that 20th-century art is ugly, but few of us, if any, can explain what we mean.

Even though our new buildings are beautiful, our new cities are not. Modern architecture has bad manners; new buildings violate the unity and tone of their neighboring communities. Our roadsides are hideous. Our suburbs, even when affluent, are drab. We know that it is too late to build a Venice or a Washington. New York, Chicago, and Hong Kong have succeeded in incorporating new structures into pre-existing plans; perhaps they are more beautiful than ever. On the other hand, cities that have been reinvented in our own time—Tokyo, Warsaw, Beijing—look like overbuilt suburbs. They too are modernist.

After modernism came post-modernism. The very name of this movement tells us that it is a rejection of reality. *Modern* by definition means "contemporary." It follows that *post-modernism* refers to something that has not yet occurred. Modernism tries to bully us and recreate us; post-modernism denies that we are real. The title and message of a play by Luigi Pirandello, *Right You Are If You Think You Are*, was a precursor of post-modernism. If the political analog of modernism is totalitarianism, then the analog of post-modernism is the suicidal cult, or Afghanistan's Taliban movement.

Yet that is only half the picture. There are lots of great musical pieces that everyone knows and loves: Debussy's *Clair de lune*, Ravel's *Bolero*, Gershwin's *Rhapsody in Blue*, Khachaturian's *Sabre Dance*, Orff's *Carmina Burana*, to name just a few. There have been musical comedies, movie scores, and several rich periods of popular music, including rock and roll. Both rock and roll and early rock music are based on simple melody lines and regular alternation of tonic and dominant chords. At least one piece, *A Lover's Concerto*, by a group called The Toys, is based on a Bach minuet.

Movie scores are not music drama but rather incidental music. Beethoven wrote music to accompany *The Ruins of Athens*, a forgotten work whose name would not even be known were it not for Beethoven's score. Schubert did the same for *Rosamunde*. Mendelssohn's *A Midsummer Night's Dream* is as well known as the play, by Shakespeare, no less. More recently, we have had Virgil Thomson's film score *Louisiana Story*, one of his beloved works. Which brings us to Erich Korngold.

Korngold (1897-1957), the subject of a biography by Brendan G. Carroll, was a child prodigy who devoted much of his career to what he called the "symphonic film score." A review of the book by Jay Nordlinger in the January 12, 1998, issue of *The Weekly Standard* tells us that at the age of 50, Korngold felt he had to leave Hollywood in order "to aim for the Pantheon of the masters," in other words, to write music that can be "studied in universities." It is both unfortunate and puzzling that serious musicians feel they have to separate themselves from popular art forms such as film, especially when we remember that movies can be as modernist and demanding as Schoenberg's serialism.

Music written to be performed in the concert hall may well have run its course. What will the music of the 21st century sound like? Terry Teachout, in the December 1997 issue of *Commentary*, writes of a new generation of American composers "influenced neither by serialism nor by minimalism but by the music of the long-unfashionable tonal modernists" (p. 56). I fear these tonal modernists will continue to be unfashionable. Tonal or atonal, minimalist or maximalist, listening to contemporary works has been identified with duty. Yet I am convinced that genius lives. Human creativity will find a new home for itself.

Chapter 11

Reconsidering *The Magic Flute*

Mozart's *The Magic Flute* is a puzzling opera. Its mood is sometimes childish, sometimes utterly solemn. The Queen of the Night is a sympathetic character who has been wronged by Sarastro when we meet her in the first act. In the second act, the situation seems reversed: Sarastro sings of wisdom, and the Queen of the Night tries vainly to persuade her daughter to commit murder. When the Queen is defeated by Sarastro at the end, the music is Mozart at his most triumphant, and the audience rejoices in the happy ending.

In my opinion, however, the ending is far from happy. I see Sarastro as a consistently villainous character, and I believe the Queen's attempt to kill him can be understood as an attempt to save her daughter from being brainwashed by the leader of a cult.

The audience sees Sarastro and the Queen through the eyes of Tamino, who is united with his beloved Pamina at the end. As for Tamino, he sees the Queen as an innocent victim when he learns that her daughter has been kidnapped by Sarastro. He goes off to rescue Pamina, but soon changes his mind about who is good and who is bad. What causes him to alter his opinion? One of Sarastro's flunkies (Sarastro is surrounded by yes-men) says to him: *"Ein Weib hat also dich berückt? Ein Weib tut wenig, plaudert viel"* (So a woman beguiled you? A woman does little, chatters a lot). Tamino, who has good intentions but is rather stupid, cannot see the fallacy of argument by appeal to prejudice. He falls for this sexist line and decides to join Sarastro's cult, the Temple of Wisdom.

Pamina, in the meantime, is being held prisoner. Sarastro has put her in the care of his faithful servant Monostatos, who *"verlangte Liebe"* (demanded love). Pamina attempts to escape and return to her mother, the Queen of the Night. Monostatos recaptures her and brings her back to Sarastro. Despite Pamina's pleas, Sarastro will not let her go. Yet Monostatos, who thwarted her attempt to flee, is sentenced to 77 lashes. Thus does Sarastro reward obedience.

This brief scene shows us just how evil Sarastro is. If he punishes Monostatos for bringing back Pamina, why must he keep her in captivity? If he disapproves of Monostatos's amorous advances, how can he put a helpless girl back into the care of this lecherous servant? Easily. He justifies it by saying that the Queen of the Night is *"ein stolzes Weib"* (a proud woman).

In an earlier scene, the Queen disciplines *her* servant, Papageno. He is punished for telling a lie by having his mouth padlocked. The punishment is very brief but effective. Papageno will never lie again. The contrast between the Queen and Sarastro is enormous. The Queen imposes a light penalty for a real offense; Monostatos, on the other hand, suffers a cruel punishment for doing precisely what Sarastro wanted done.

Let us get back to Tamino. In order to join the Temple of Wisdom, he will have to pass the test of silence. The test is singularly inappropriate. Wisdom is the result of knowledge, questioning, and discussion. Only through argument can our views be subject to scrutiny. Silence is the enemy of wisdom; it is a virtue only in a totalitarian regime like Sarastro's. Tamino, then, must be silent when Pamina is brought to him. She mistakes his silence for rejection and attempts suicide. Sarastro, who organized this cruel test, does nothing to aid Pamina, who is not even being tested. Instead she is saved by the Genii, who are spirits sent by the Queen of the Night to guide Tamino. The Genii, like the magic bells and the magic flute that gives the opera its name, are gifts of the Queen. They are forces for good throughout the opera. In fact, when Pamina and Tamino undergo the tests of fire and water, devised by Sarastro, they are protected by the flute, the instrument of the Queen.

The Queen, to be sure, has her villainous moment. When she learns that Tamino, her daughter's beloved, has joined Sarastro, she becomes desperate. She gives Pamina a dagger and tells her to kill Sarastro. The Queen has been driven mad by the hopelessness of her situation. Her action is futile: Pamina will not be able to commit the murder.

It is at this point that the Queen sings her glorious aria *"Der Hölle Rache kocht in meinem Herzen"* (The wrath of Hell boils in my heart). The music is so wonderful that we know the Queen's rage must be justified. Sarastro's music, to be sure, is also wonderful. Mozart didn't write bad music. It is therefore quite significant that there is no music at all, except for some trumpet blasts, during the tedious scene where Sarastro announces Tamino's wish to join the Temple. Similarly, there is only dialogue when Tamino and Papageno are asked if they wish to take the tests (Papageno sensibly declines). Mozart was just not inspired to compose music for these sequences.

Did Mozart and his librettist, Emanuel Schikaneder, know what they were doing? Did they fail to see that Sarastro was a tyrant? Did they agree with the sexism, gross even by 18th-century standards, expressed by Sarastro and his toadies? I do not know. Pamina and Tamino are together at the end of the opera, and to that extent the opera ends happily. They will live under a dictatorship, but their love will make their problems irrelevant. Pamina will forget her mother, who is destroyed despite Sarastro's claim that vengeance is unknown in his realm.

Whatever Mozart's intentions, audiences have always sided with Sarastro. In Ingmar Bergman's movie version of the opera, the singer who plays the Queen is shown smoking under a no-smoking sign during the intermission. Bergman, like most of us, has misjudged the Queen. The time has come for her to be recognized as the tragic heroine she really is.

Chapter 12

Reconsidering *Così Fan Tutte*

"This world is a comedy to those that think, a tragedy to those that feel," said Horace Walpole. *Così fan tutte* is certainly a comedy. Its librettist, Lorenzo Da Ponte, was a man who thought; its composer, Mozart, was without any question a man who felt. Da Ponte was a genius, but *Così fan tutte* is performed and loved today because the greatest of all geniuses, Mozart, gave us its music— music that at times is comic, at times light, but at other times passionate and profound.

Così fan tutte means "so do they all," with *tutte* (all) in the feminine. What is it that they all do? Don Alfonso, the cynical baritone who organizes the practical joke that forms the plot of the opera, thinks he knows what all women do: they are fickle. To prove his point, he persuades the heroes of the opera, Ferrando and Guglielmo, to leave their fiancées, return in disguise, and steal the hearts of Dorabella and Fiordiligi away from the men they are engaged to marry.

This is the kind of nasty plot that is typical of the comedies of the 17th and 18th centuries, a plot involving disguise and deception, in which the reality of human emotion is denied and mocked. Contemporary audiences generally dislike comedies of this period—after all, there is more feeling as well as more humor in an *I Love Lucy* rerun.

The early scenes of *Così fan tutte* are standard 18th-century comedy. Guglielmo tells us his beloved is perfection, the phoenix: "La fenice è Fiordiligi." Ferrando thinks it is *his* fiancée: "Dorabella è la fenice." Neither the music nor the words suggest men in love; what we hear instead is fun and energy.

Ferrando and Guglielmo, who have been teased by Don Alfonso into going along with his gag, pretend to leave for war. They come back wearing ridiculous disguises and proceed to woo the ladies. It is not clear at this point which gentleman is after which lady, but the way they go about showing their love is by pretending to commit suicide. They are "saved" by the maid, Despina, who disguises herself as a doctor and cures them with a giant magnet. All in good fun.

In Act I, there are solo arias, duets, trios, sextets, and a chorus. One thing is missing: there are no love duets. Nowhere in the opera does Ferrando sing a love duet with Dorabella, nor does Fiordiligi ever sing a duet with Guglielmo. Why should they? They don't love each other. If they did, it would break the mood. There is no place for love in 18th-century comedy.

Something significant happens in Act II. The young women do not recognize their disguised lovers, but there is a different thing they recognize. They know which of the two they prefer: neither prefers her finacé! Dorabella will take the dark one: "Prenderò quel brunettino." Fiordiligi likes the blond one, "il biondino." Dorabella, the mezzo, has chosen Guglielmo, the bass. Fiordiligi, the soprano, likes Ferrando, the tenor. The situation at the beginning was all wrong. Can a mezzo ever wind up with a tenor? Ridiculous.

Not too much further into the second act, Guglielmo and Dorabella sing a duet, "Il core vi dono" (I give you my heart). It is the first male-female duet in *Così fan tutte*. We can hear the hearts beating in the words and in the music: "Perche batte batte batte qui?" (Why is it beating beating beating here?). In literature, when we say two hearts are beating as one, it is merely a figure of speech. In music, we hear it; we feel it; we know it has to be true. This love duet is one of the most beautiful in all opera. But it is more than that. It is also the most convincing. The music has taken us from the coldness of comedy to the warmth of love.

When the women fall in love, they become real. Each has her own personality. Dorabella has given in to her passion. Fiordiligi cannot come to terms with her emotions. Her great second-act aria, "Per pieta," is filled with doubt and turmoil. When Fiordiligi finally surrenders to Ferrando, it is not because she is fickle. She has found the great love of her life. She tried to be loyal to Guglielmo as long as possible, but she failed. Besides, Guglielmo never deserved her loyalty, nor did Ferrando merit devotion from Dorabella. Both men had casually agreed to play Don Alfonso's game. The initial pairings were wrong from the start.

Don Alfonso has won his bet. He makes Guglielmo and Ferrando sing after him "Così fan tutte," to the notes E F A D E. We heard almost the same theme in the overture: E F A D G E, a sequence of half notes, marked *andante*. It is neither a light nor a comic melody. Rather, it sounds solemn, almost ominous. Is that the appropriate music for asserting that women are fickle and love is a joke?

At the end of the opera, the disguises are taken off and the lovers are married. Who marries whom? The libretto does not say. The silence of the text suggests that we go back to the beginning: Ferrando with Dorabella, Guglielmo with Fiordiligi. That is the way the final scene is usually staged. It is in keeping with the comic mood of the opera, the traditions of the times, and probably the intentions of the composer and librettist.

Once in a great while, the final scene is done differently, and the women get to marry the men they have fallen in love with. That is the way it ought to be. We know, because the music has told us so, that Fiordiligi loves Ferrando and Dorabella loves Guglielmo. We know, because the music has told us so, that their love is real. We know that if they went back to their original fiancés, the men would forever resent the women for their betrayal, and the women would hate the men for the cruelty of their joke.

If women are indeed fickle, why should Fiordiligi and Dorabella show loyalty to their original fiancés? If women are capable of true lasting love, then why shouldn't they stay with the men they love? The answer usually given is that the opera isn't about real people, that it is a comedy not to be taken seriously. The problem is caused by Mozart's greatness. He was too good a composer; his music has too much feeling to go with such a silly story. The title, *Così fan tutte*, says that women's emotions are not real. Mozart's music proves that the title is wrong.

Chapter 13

Reconsidering Shakespeare

What is the worst play ever written? Literary critics and scholars may nominate a host of works unknown to the general reader. For a layperson, however, all the contenders for this distinction are by Shakespeare: *Cymbeline, Love's Labour's Lost, All's Well That Ends Well, The Winter's Tale, Much Ado About Nothing, Two Gentlemen of Verona.* These works are badly constructed, unfunny, dull, and disagreeable. Homer sometimes nods; certainly Hamlet does not belong in the same category as these comedies. It is natural for the poor works of a famous author to bask in the glow of the better works. Nevertheless, it is puzzling that the world respects and—even more surprising—reads these failures.

Shakespeare's comedies are morally obtuse—works in which evil behavior is presented as good. We can't be sure that Shakespeare thought teasing, insulting, and practical joking were beautiful, or even morally neutral, although he must have thought they were funny. Be that as it may, the teasers, ruse players and insulters are the heroes. Audiences like Petruchio and Puck.

Comedies are typically bound to their own time and place; tragedy is universal. I remember when I first saw Mozart's *Marriage of Figaro*, at the age of 15. The performance was in English, and I hadn't read the libretto. The surprises in the plot all worked for me. It was the funniest thing I had ever seen. I later was told that for political reasons, Mozart's librettist, Lorenzo Da Ponte, had cut out all the really good lines, so I went to read the original play by Beaumarchais. I found the lines, but the play was not especially funny. The opera has survived but not the play (except in graduate school). Music, like tragedy, transcends time and place. Music can carry even comedy along with it. Shakespeare's music—his language—together with his fame, helped to carry his comedies into our own century.

Comedy is frequently based on cruelty and insult. Prince Hal regularly teases his friend Falstaff in the two Henry IV plays by calling him fat and cowardly. When Malvolio, in *Twelfth Night*, commits the sin of falling in love, he is sent to jail as part of a practical joke. The comedy of *The Comedy of Errors* is the result of the servants getting beaten because of mistaken identity. All of this is supposed to be very funny. There is no place for patience or soft-heartedness here.

The few characters in Shakespeare who merit our sympathy are victims. We are moved by the tragedy of Romeo and Juliet, who are destroyed by the callousness of their families. Juliet's mother, Lady Capulet, shows no emotion for her daughter until Juliet declines to marry the man her father has chosen. Then we see what the mother thinks of her daughter: "I would the fool were married to her grave" (Act 3, sc. 5). Juliet's father is even more hostile:

> Wife, we scarce thought us blest
> That God had lent us but this only child;
> But now I see this one is too much,
> And that we have a curse in having her.
> (Act 3, sc. 5)

The Nurse is Juliet's ally and friend. Yet when Juliet is desperate for news about Romeo, the Nurse teases her unmercifully by holding back the information: "Can you not stay awhile? Do you not see that I am out of breath?"

> How art thou out of breath when thou hast breath
> To say to me that thou art out of breath?
> (Act 2, sc. 5)

replies Juliet, indignant that the Nurse is playing with her. But that is how characters act in Shakespeare.

There are two types of society where rudeness is the norm: the worlds of chivalry and of hooliganism. The fact that the plot of *Romeo and Juliet* was so successfully adapted as *West Side Story* is an illustration of the similarities between knighthood and gang membership. Both are reflections of the values of machismo: courage, toughness, and willingness to fight on the one hand; loyalty to family and community on the other. There is no place for outsiders. As for women, they may be protected or exploited or loved, but their loyalty is to their men and not directly to the community and its values.

It is normal for such a society to value rudeness, especially to outsiders. Hostility keeps alien elements away and provokes fights, enabling the knights and hooligans to test their courage. A headline in the *New York Times* on March 11, 1997: "Man Charged and Motive Cited in Bayonne School Stabbings." Under the headline, we read: "A 20-year-old man was arrested today and charged with fatally stabbing Bayonne High School student and wounding another last week after a chance hallway encounter led to an argument over 'the way people were looking at and talking to each other,' the authorities said." We are reminded of a dialogue in Act 1, Sc. 1 of *Romeo and Juliet*, where Abraham, a servant to Montague, and Sampson, a servant to Capulet, mimic the feuds of their bosses:

> Abraham: Do you bite your thumb at us, sir?
> Sampson: I do bite my thumb, sir.

Characters in Shakespeare plays may do good because of love, loyalty, family, friendship, etc. But there is no common decency in Shakespeare. When one character encounters another with whom there is no special bond of interest or loyalty, the only behavior we find is teasing, either in the form of vicious practical jokes or abuse by means of puns. In other words, there is hooliganism—the code of chivalry and the street gang, the world where insensitivity and violence define masculinity—the world that has been reincarnated as fascism and ultranationalism.

On Friday July 12, 1991, the film *Boyz N the Hood* opened, and riots broke out at movie theaters across the nation. A man was fatally shot in Riverdale, Illinois; another was stabbed in Commack, Long Island. According to a news story in the July 14, 1991, issue of *The New York Times* ("An Anti-Gang Movie Opens to Violence"), "There had been concern in many cities that the film would attract rival gang members, and that rival gangs in close proximity would inevitably mean violence."

Why inevitably? Because to get to the theater, gang members had to cross into the territories of other gangs. "If every gang territory had its own movie house we would not have a problem," says Steve Valdivia, executive director of Community Youth Gang Services, according to the *Times*. And why should gangs have territories where others may not pass? Why should there be gangs at all?

"That is the question," said Hamlet. He was talking about a different question, suicide. But the question he should have asked himself is why he was so horribly rude, especially to Ophelia. When Hamlet was able to act decisively, he too was a hooligan, quick on the draw, who killed the wrong man by accident.

Miguel de Cervantes (1547-1616) was a contemporary of Shakespeare's (1564-1616). Cervantes' *Don Quixote*, who thought he was a knight but was merely a hooligan, subscribed to the values of chivalry and traveled around looking for a fight. He was always defeated, even by the windmills he attacked, and the other characters in *Don Quixote* refer to him as crazy. Don Quixote was indeed delusional; the adjective "quixotic" doesn't apply to him. He persisted in clinging to the rules of an earlier age, which had been rejected during the Renaissance because the rules themselves were crazy.

People communicate by talking. If they can't believe each other, they can't test their own internal reality against that of the outside world. In other words, they are crazy. Hamlet is a character who cannot tell the truth; consequently, he cannot expect it in return, nor can he recognize it. Instead of conversations he has games of wit. Few Shakespeare characters ever use the truth as a weapon. Instead, they devise ridiculous schemes to uncover falsehood (the play's the thing). Othello never tries to have a conversation with Desdemona in which he lets her talk; he doesn't (and probably couldn't) understand the need to show the evidence to the accused. A world that has dismissed the idea of honest investigation, that thinks that words can only deceive and never inform, is a crazy world. Worse than that, it is a world that has rejected science—human curiosity, the moral imperative to learn.

Hamlet pretends to be crazy; he will "put an antic disposition on" (Act 1, Sc. 5). The audience can never learn to what extent he really is insane, since the society itself has rejected honest communication. Unlike Don Quixote, who is a surviving relic of a mad culture, Hamlet's Denmark is itself mad, committed to chivalry and machismo.

Without the ghost, neither Hamlet nor anyone else (with the exception of Claudius, if he is indeed guilty) suspects murder. There seems to have been no reason to do so. Can it be that Hamlet is clinically psychotic and is just hearing voices from speakers implanted in his teeth by the CIA? We don't know enough about the pre-antic-disposition Hamlet to come to a conclusion. Is his conversation with the ghost—in private—evidence of his insanity? That might make the play a better one. Introducing the supernatural into an otherwise natural work always cheapens it.

Hamlet, a prince and therefore raised to be a hooligan, doesn't feel guilty about accidentally killing a bystander, even when it turns out to be his girlfriend's father. Hamlet can't for the life of him understand why Laertes is peeved about the death of Polonius, although you'd think he would know from experience that there are those who get annoyed when their fathers are murdered. Sensitivity, like morality, cannot exist without communication. There is only one moment when Hamlet hesitates: when he catches Claudius praying. The play is not about indecision but about investigation. But where there is no truth, there can be no knowledge.

Loyalty is the glue that holds feudal societies and street gangs together. Loyalty to whom? To the legitimate ruler. For Shakespeare, legitimate monarchies ruled by strong kings can control evil but never eliminate it. The only human institution that Shakespeare respects is legitimacy, which depends upon the rules of succession. The moral of the *Henry IV* tetralogy seems to be that it is wrong to usurp the throne, but the son of a usurper is a legitimate heir. On the other hand, the *Henry VI* tetralogy, written earlier but describing a later time in history, shows how the weak grandson of a usurper is overthrown because his grandfather's crime is used against him. The Wars of the Roses, both as historical occurrences and as the subject of Shakespeare's plays, show how monarchy is an inherently unstable form of government. Kings enforce order among their subjects, but are not themselves bound by law. Shakespeare could understand neither law nor society. He is a monarchist because monarchy is the least political form of politics.

Shakespeare couldn't have known that only in a democracy is there the possibility of a ruler being subject to law. Nor could he have known that democracy is inherently stable, despite his preoccupation with the legitimate order. But he knew enough about democracy to attack it in *Julius Caesar* by showing how the mob could be manipulated. It is interesting that in the Roman plays, there is little lying. Shakespeare recognized that ancient Rome was a pre-chivalry society, where honest communication was possible. Nevertheless, his plays are about dishonest worlds, since only democracy is inherently honest.

To the extent that Shakespeare defines himself as a political writer, he has little to say that shows respect for the dignity of the individual and the species.

Shakespeare, to be sure, never told us exactly what he thought, since he was speaking through his characters and his plots. Did he really think that lying and ruses were good? We can't exclude beyond a doubt the possibility that he was merely saying that this is the way people behave. But he never presents an alternative.

For Shakespeare, Christianity was legitimate, and Judaism therefore was not. Mercy, viewed as Christian, was good; justice, viewed as Jewish, was bad. Justice and mercy were somehow considered mutually exclusive. "The quality of mercy is not strained" is perhaps the most famous line in *The Merchant of Venice*. Yet in all of Shakespeare's dramas, is there—anywhere—a character who shows mercy to another?

Shylock, like Caliban and Malvolio, belongs to an outcast category. Legitimate characters in Shakespeare's plays abuse and insult these pariahs as a matter of course. Shylock is unique not because of his callousness—who is more hardhearted than Hamlet is to Ophelia?—but because his villainy, natural as it may be to a Shakespearean Jew, is well motivated. We may hate Shylock, but we understand his rage as we can never really understand the anger of Iago, or even the hostility of Beatrice and Benedick. *The Merchant of Venice* is a popular play because Shylock is the most psychologically plausible of Shakespeare's villains.

Tragedy is not inherently pessimistic. Sophocles' plays show that there are conflicting rights and conflicting values (*Antigone*), and that we may do harm by trying to do good (*Oedipus*). These ideas are the basis for free thought and rule of law. The past is another country, and so is Greece. Yet Sophocles is our contemporary and our fellow American.

Should art improve the world? Certainly: by being great art. Shakespeare gave us great art in his poetry. He did the same when he created an interesting character, like Shylock, who will always inspire interest and disagreement; or an interesting situation, like the one in Julius Caesar; or portrayed suffering human beings, like Desdemona and Romeo and Juliet. He failed when his characters, like Hamlet, were too stupid and too unfeeling for us to identify with them. Wherever his plays are morally obtuse and therefore boring, Shakespeare fails as an artist. His failures outnumber his successes.

Chapter 14

Reconsidering Dark Restaurants

When people are intelligent, we call them bright; when they are stupid, we call them dim or dull. People have always associated light with intelligence. We give our children names like Claire and Clara, both of which mean "bright." In China, the same thing happens. Children are sometimes named Ming, meaning "bright."

Darkness is associated with evil; Satan is the Prince of Darkness. Stupidity—dimness—is like evil because it keeps us from seeing clearly. Clarity, needless to say, comes from a Latin word meaning "light" or "bright."

Restaurants are getting better all the time. New York is a particular showplace for this phenomenon. Food is more varied and interesting—and delicious—than ever before. Nevertheless, for the last 15 or 20 years, restaurants have been undoing their excellence by getting darker.

This is especially surprising when we stop to think that food is not merely delicious but also beautiful to look at. Chefs decorate their creations, especially their desserts. Food that looks good automatically tastes better. Designing food to look beautiful and then turning down the lights is the essence of dim-wittedness.

People are beautiful. Some are more beautiful than others, but all are beautiful. We like to go to restaurants with other people. We want to talk to them and see them. If the surroundings are too dark, we can't see them very well. Even talking gets harder, since we can't altogether read the expressions on the faces of our companions.

Darkness is romantic, I have been told. I don't agree. We associate darkness with romance because romantic moments often take place in the dark. Clarity and understanding are even more romantic. Understanding our fellow human beings is romantic, and understanding requires light—honesty.

Restaurants weren't always dark. I first became aware of dark restaurants when my family and I took a trip through the Midwest in 1967 and ate in motel dining rooms. The dim lighting was a mistaken attempt at achieving elegance. Eventually, this silly practice spread. It is now almost universal in New York. It hasn't yet taken over Paris, that most delicious of cities, but it probably will.

Fads have their own strength. The playwright Eugene Ionesco depicted the power—and the danger—of fads in his comedy *Rhinoceros*. There is a Yiddish proverb that warns us against fads: *Eyn nar makht a sakh naronim*, which means "One fool makes many fools," or in my father's brilliant translation, "One stupid makes a lot of stupids."

What are the first words that God ever says? "Let there be light" (Gen. 1:3). Light is creation. Light is the Big Bang. "And God saw the light, that it was good" (Gen. 1:4). Restaurants have forgotten that light is good. They have fallen from grace.

Chapter 15

Reconsidering Tipping

Tipping is not confined to restaurants. By its nature, it spreads. It is a custom that can lead to confusion. Let me tell you about an experience of mine to show how far it can reach.

In 1989, when I was teaching in China, I went to Shanxi Province in order to visit the parents of a friend of mine. My friend's mother was in the hospital. His father invited my daughter and me to an elegant restaurant for dinner. He also invited the doctors who were treating his wife. He explained that it was customary to give gifts to one's physician.

Tipping a doctor! What a horrible idea. How much do you tip? How do you go about tipping? What if the doctor doesn't enjoy the dinner you've invited him to?

Why do we tip? Does tipping improve service? I doubt it; if it did, taxi drivers would be more courteous than flight attendants. Furthermore, tipping is undignified, since blurring the line between a fee and a gift puts both patron and server in a vulnerable position.

Restaurant employees should certainly be able to earn as much money as they get from their salaries and their tips combined. Restaurants should raise their prices, pay their waiters more, and put the words "no tipping" on all checks and menus. If they did, dining would be a more elegant experience.

In America we don't tip physicians. If we live in apartment houses, however, we have to tip our supers. Let me tell you about another experience of mine. A UPS (United Parcel Service) man rang my bell bringing a package for apartment 5G, two doors from mine. I was surprised but accepted it. I put a note under 5G's door. Later I ran into the super's mother and told her about it. "5G don't take care of Louie, Louie don't take care of her," said the super's mother.

Poor 5G. She never learned that she was being punished. We human beings can—sometimes—learn from our experiences. We can't learn, however, if we don't know what is causing the unfortunate consequences. The punishment is not a lesson when we don't know that it is in fact punishment.

New York draws residents from out of town and out of the country. How are they to know about the necessity of giving Christmas presents when New

Yorkers themselves are not sure? How can you play by the rules if the rules are a secret?

A present is not the same thing as a transaction. It is a simple act of generosity or friendship or love. Giving is not the same thing as trading. Services should be paid for; gifts are gifts, not payment.

There are always new places where tipping is expected. Why should we have to leave a tip when we stand at a counter and wait to be served a cappuccino? Will stores be next? Or will the day come, in our ever more money-oriented world, when we will have to worry about how much to tip the doctor?

Chapter 16

Reconsidering Wasting Food

Children are an oppressed minority. They are physically weak, unable to seek legal assistance, and unable to build organizations. Furthermore, they are dependent upon grownups for their survival, which makes them a burden to those who care for them.

One of the ways that parents oppress children is by coaxing and sometimes forcing them to eat. My aunts—not my parents—all forced their children to eat, and it was an upsetting sight to behold. One of my aunts put food into her daughter's mouth and held it closed until she swallowed.

My parents certainly believed that a fat child was healthier than a thin one. They were under great pressure from my aunts and uncles to make me eat more, not simply to make me fatter but for reasons of discipline. But they saw what nobody else was able to see, even though the evidence was before their eyes: coaxing children to eat is unpleasant for the parents and unkind to the child.

My aunt who held her daughter's mouth closed was a warm, good-natured woman who loved her children very much. But she was under pressure from society, and she didn't realize she was being cruel. This type of pressure no longer exists among middle-class parents, but it remains the rule among the poor, immigrants, and minorities—the groups most plagued by obesity.

Obesity is plaguing the nation. Nevertheless, parents still teach their children to finish the food placed in front of them. This makes no sense.

When I was a child, when obesity was rare among children, I was encouraged by the various people who took care of me to finish the food on my plate. "Think of the starving children in Europe," I was told.

"Mail them my food," I replied.

"You think you're funny," I was told. I eventually internalized the habit of finishing what was on my plate. Over the years, I gained a lot of weight. When I felt full at mealtime, even though I knew I was overweight, I consumed what was in front of me. Perhaps that is why I had to undergo coronary bypass surgery in 1991.

When I was four or five, I hated fat and tried to cut it off my meat. "It's the best part," I was told. Once a doctor suggested to my parents that I wouldn't be so thin if I ate bacon. Bacon had never entered our Jewish home, but Jewish law teaches that saving a life takes precedence over other religious laws. The bacon smelled delicious, but it tasted like fat. Is there a doctor anywhere today who thinks that bacon is necessary to save a thin child's health? Nobody seems to know what the Bible says: "It shall be a perpetual statute throughout your generations in all your dwellings, that ye shall eat neither fat nor blood" (Lev. 3:17).

Human beings, like all living creatures, were designed to survive. We get hungry because we need food; we feel full when we don't need food. Grownups systematically teach children to disregard the messages that their bodies send them. Everywhere in the world, children learn to ignore natural feelings of satiety. As grownups, they cannot lose this unnaturally acquired insensitivity.

Nevertheless, we were designed to be sensitive to feelings of satiety. There is a hormone that causes full feelings. It is called PYY, and researchers are working on pills that may be used in the future to control obesity. In theory, we should not need pills. Our own bodies produce PYY. If we hadn't been trained as children to ignore what our bodies told us, our own PYY would be enough to keep us in shape.

My own parents were kind, generous people who loved me. They were not the principal villains. The problem was the whole world. Teachers, relatives, neighbors, friends—all were conspirators in a plot to teach me to eat more. "Try it; you'll like it." My favorite food was spinach, but there was a universal conspiracy to teach me that dessert was best. "If you don't finish your vegetables, you won't get dessert," said the world. There were other parents who were really major offenders. A friend of mine told me recently that his mother made him eat the food he had spit up.

My parents worked in the defense industry, making airplane parts. Their work week was long—it was during World War II—and I was left with a woman named Charlotte. Nowadays she would be called a nanny, but I never heard that word in the 1940s. I was terrified of her. One day she was trying to get me to eat some potatoes, which I hated. I told her my mother didn't make me eat things I didn't like.

"You're lying," she said.

"I'll call my mother. She'll tell you." I didn't think Charlotte would allow me to go to the phone, but she did. She must have been sure my mother would back her up. My mother asked me to put Charlotte on the phone. After the conversation, Charlotte took away the potatoes. She never made me look at a potato again. My mother was obviously a brilliant, creative thinker. There were very few parents in the 1940s who could possibly have known that it was wrong to force children to eat. My mother felt quite insecure about the fact that she didn't make me eat. Like her contemporaries, she didn't know that fat was unhealthy. But she, and my father, knew that force-feeding was cruel. Since my parents knew this, so did I. I could see how nasty my aunts were being to my cousins three times a day.

The grownups who tell their children to eat have nothing to gain. In 1937, when I was born, a plump child was considered healthier than a thin one, as is shown by the story of the doctor who recommended bacon. A few decades ago, when, most probably, force feeding was a great deal more common than it is now, parents thought it was for the child's good. Parents who make an issue of food nowadays don't even have the excuse of health to back them up. Then why do they do it? Lack of originality.

The thirties and forties were the years when parents used to let their helpless babies scream rather than give them milk between their regular four-hour feedings. Letting babies go hungry while force feeding toddlers showed a certain inconsistency, but both reflected a fear of spoiling children. How this parental nastiness protected children from being spoiled and just what was meant by spoiling are unclear. However, I do remember hearing people ask my parents, in my presence, "Is he a good boy? Does he eat?"

I am no longer a boy, but I certainly eat. Even when I am full, my hunger remains unsatisfied. Years of pressure damaged my body's natural signals. Years of education taught me not to waste food. I know, consciously, that eating what you neither need nor want is wasting it. My conscious mind, alas, is too weak to overcome my conditioning.

"But if children don't eat at mealtime, they will get hungry between meals," say parents. So what? Keep lots of carrots, apples and yogurt in the house. Moderately enlightened parents, who claim they would never force feed their children, instead tempt them or encourage them to clean their plates. In terms of health, coaxing is no better than forcing. Overeating is overeating.

God, in His wisdom, gave our bodies PYY to help us distinguish between hunger and satisfaction. Human beings, in their ingenuity, created the garbage can. Parents should accept these gifts with gratitude. If they do, perhaps, fifty years from now, their children won't need bypass surgery. Even if health weren't an issue, children, like all human beings, should not be oppressed.

Chapter 17

Reconsidering Santa Claus

Christmas is a beautiful holiday. One aspect of its beauty is the custom of exchanging gifts. It is wonderful to have an excuse to give presents to those we love—generosity is something we find embarrassing if there is no occasion for it. It is especially pleasurable for parents to give Christmas presents to their children and for children to receive them.

Yet parents, almost universally, lie to their young children about Christmas. They say the gifts come from Santa Claus, who lives in a cold climate but has a warm heart. I cannot imagine why parents choose to depersonalize Christmas in this way. Isn't it better to get presents from Mommy and Daddy instead of from some remote philanthropist whose benevolence extends to millions of children? Or is it benevolence? Our popular music tells us that "he's making a list and checking it twice. He's gonna find out who's naughty or nice." The gifts are not gifts at all; they are positive reinforcement. And who is this man who "knows if you've been bad or good, so be good for goodness' sake"? A walking data bank!

Children, like all human beings, should be treated with respect. When we consider their ignorance adorable, we are using them as playthings and depriving them of their dignity. The business of children is learning about the world. It is a job that can never be completed. The business of a parent is helping a child to grow up—to learn what reality is and how to deal with it. When a parent lies to a child, the essential role of parenthood is subverted.

Sooner or later, the truth must come out. No one can grow up and still believe in Santa Claus. Finding out that there is no Santa Claus is not only disappointing but destructive. The child learns that the parents are morally flawed—guilty of pointless falsehood. Perhaps our society would be less cynical if parents were more honest.

Once there was a little girl named Virginia who asked, "Is there a Santa Claus?" It was a simple, touching question. She wanted a simple, honest answer. Nobody could give it to her.

Chapter 18

Reconsidering Sports

There is nothing wrong with playing sports. Nor is there anything wrong with watching sports; it is always a pleasure to see things well done. But there is something mysteriously wrong about rooting for a team.

Soccer riots are an obvious example of the dangers of supporting one's team too enthusiastically. People have been killed in soccer riots. It doesn't make sense to celebrate a victory or mourn a defeat with violence. But does it make sense to celebrate a victory or mourn a defeat at all? What has been won or lost? Pride? Why should the accomplishments of professional athletes be a source of pride? Who are we to them or they to us?

They seem to be our country, our city, our school. Team loyalty mirrors other forms of loyalty, nationalism in particular. Team games are symbolic wars. Nationalism is one of the strongest emotions. When nationalism goes wrong, as it so often does, it is a force of great destruction. Games, on the other hand, are just that: games. When countries fight, they kill. Victory and defeat mean everything, including life and death, to the warring sides. At games, where victory and defeat mean nothing at all, the emotional involvement is as great as in a war. That makes no sense.

Logical or not, it shouldn't matter if people invest their emotions in unimportant things. If one's honor or self-esteem is bound up with irrelevant factors, so be it. Everyone should have the right to be interested in whatever they want to be. If people want to root for their teams, they shouldn't have to prove that victory is important. If they consider it important, then it is important to them.

But there is a problem. Too much of the world's corruption, too much of its violence is linked to sports. In America, universities are under pressure to violate their own rules for the sake of their teams. The world is kind to athletes. "Kindness" may be the wrong word. The world, or at least certain segments of it, approves of violence when committed by athletes. Why did so many people support American athlete O. J. Simpson when he was charged with murder? Why was Simpson different from any other person charged with two sordid crimes? Because he is an athlete, that's why. Rules of morality are threatened by the corruption surrounding the world of sports. Why is so much attention lavished on sports? Sports don't matter.

Is there something corrupting about being interested in the unimportant? Offhand, the answer should be no. Perhaps gambling is the link. Gambling—making or hoping to make large sums of money without providing goods or services—has often attracted criminals. Yet there is nothing inherently dishonest about gambling. For that matter, there is nothing inherently antisocial about sports.

The world is filled with violence and dishonesty, most of it in no way connected to sports. Most sports fans—and most people are sports fans—are a normal cross-section of humanity. Most games end without violence. Most athletes do not play dirty. What, then, can be wrong about rooting for one's team?

But think. Would the crowds that lined the roads to cheer for O. J. Simpson as he was attempting to escape to Mexico before his trial have done so had he merely been a singer or actor or politician? Of course not. Sports are a phenomenon that makes smart people stupid.

Chapter 19

Reconsidering Gay
and Jewish Success

Comparing Jews to homosexuals is like comparing apples and oranges—it is an enjoyable game and may lead to interesting insights. Apples and oranges may be compared for sweetness, acidity, weight per unit volume, ease of peeling, etc. Jews and homosexuals are comparable because they are unpopular minorities. There is at least one way, however, in which the comparisons are not analogous: an orange can never be an apple, but a Jew may turn out to be a fruit.

There is nothing especially surprising about the unpopularity of a minority. Xenophobia is a ubiquitous human phenomenon. People dislike those who differ from them in religion, ethnicity, accent, class, age, politics, and even taste. It would be odd if homosexuals and Jews were not disliked. As it happens, *dislike* is too mild a word. Homophobia and anti-Semitism are among the great hatreds of all time. Members of both groups, during certain periods, have been killed simply for being what they are. Even in good times, they are accused of clannishness and flaunting their differences when they stick with their own, and are considered dishonest and even insidious when they try to be like the majority.

It is much easier for Jews and gays to pass than it is for blacks, but passing is not the same as changing one's status. Gays who lead exclusively heterosexual lives know that inside, they are still fags or dykes. Karl Marx was a baptized Lutheran as well as an atheist, but everyone thought of him and thinks of him as a Jew. For both Jews and gays, conversion is possible and sometimes quite practical. One may change one's belief, affiliation, and way of life. But to oneself and the enemy (and there are so many enemies) the change is irrelevant. It may even be used as an argument to justify prejudice: They are everywhere. You don't know who they are. They control everything.

Jews and gays do not control everything. One of the striking similarities they share is that they have a great deal of influence but very little power—a sure formula for disaster. In recent years, both have become more powerful through organization and boldness. If either Jews or gays had been as militant in 1944 as they are today, the United States would have bombed the gas chambers and crematoria at Auschwitz.

Pianists are frequently gay; violinists are often Jews. Homosexuals and Jews seem to be overrepresented in the arts, show business, the garment industry, the university, and to judge by the shops in gay neighborhoods, in retail trades. Both groups do well in school and at their jobs, yet both are particularly subject to doubt and depression.

Much has been written about the reasons for Jewish success. Let me add my own theory. Jews do well for the same reason that male homosexuals do: they have escaped the subculture of adolescent men. Jews, like gay men, are successful because they are not macho.

Young males are dangerous. They are responsible for much more than their share of auto accidents, crimes of violence, and anti-social behavior in general. Peer-group pressure, especially among the lower classes, leads young men to be ashamed of their intellectual and artistic abilities. Sensitivity and original thinking are condemned as effeminate. In extreme cases, the peer group demands senseless acts of courage—in the suburbs, cars are usually involved; in the slums, crime may be the way to prove one's manhood. More often, the subculture is relatively benign. Yet even then, it works against expressing one's feelings and developing one's thoughts.

Gay young men are not likely to adopt the mores of male subcultures, which enforce their rules by calling deviants "fag." Homosexuality, evidence suggests, is determined long before the teen years. Even before a gay boy learns he is a homosexual, he knows he is somehow different. He does not feel at ease with tough males, and the feeling is mutual.

Among Jews, the traditional roles for men and women have worked to the advantage of both women and men. Women, more often than in most traditional societies, were bread-winners. This was especially true when their husbands were scholars. Study of the Bible and Talmud was restricted to men: thus it was never considered effeminate to spend one's time talking, reading, and thinking. Maleness was not equated with toughness. The way to be macho was to be skillful at explicating a text. This was so despite the fact that only a small minority of Jews were full-time scholars. Talmud study hardly survived among secular Jews. There is no direct connection between the scholarship of traditional Jews and the fact that secular Jews do well in school. The link is an indirect one: Jews did not and do not think that real men were supposed to be insensitive and stupid. This attitude has remained and has kept many Jewish men—not all—from adopting the values of the male adolescent subculture.

When Jewish women went to work to support their scholar husbands, they probably considered it oppressive rather than liberating, and with good reason. It *was* oppressive. Since there were few full-time scholars, there were few wives of such scholars. Nevertheless, women were shown to be capable. They did not need men to bring home the bacon—uh, the pastrami. Ironically, the sharply divided sex roles of a traditional society equipped Jewish women and Jewish men to cope with the changing, complex structures of contemporary America.

Neither Jews nor homosexuals are dangerous. If there are many of them in the arts and the professions, that is a plus, not a minus. They are probably more law-abiding than the population at large, except, of course, where it is against the law to be gay or Jewish. It is simply not true that Jews are more likely than others to be dishonest businesspeople. Many Jews don't even like business and typically abandon their family enterprises to go into the professions. Nor is it true that homosexuals can tempt heterosexual youths into following a gay life style. Homosexuality is not appealing to those who are not inclined that way.

Despite the fact that many gays and Jews succeed economically and intellectually, and despite the fact that they are more readily accepted than before, they remain marginal groups. No one was ever raised to be a homosexual. People who realize they are gay must either fight their own natures or live unconventional lives or both. Jews, unlike gays, may have been raised to be Jews. Yet every Jew, like every gay, must make a decision about how to reconcile the value of the larger society with the contrary needs of the particular in one's own life. A personal crisis involving a conflict between one's essence and the surrounding culture can be a radicalizing experience. It is not surprising that Jews and gays are disproportionately involved in leftist activity.

Ironically, leftist activism can help Jews and gays only in a bourgeois democracy. Democratic states have been quite hostile to minorities, yet such societies are committed in theory to pluralism. When the minorities organize to improve their positions, they have the professed values of the state on their side. As marginal groups gain in power, they gain respectability as well. As society grows more democratic in practice, people begin to understand and believe the theory of pluralism.

All societies that claim to be radical are either Marxist-Leninist or Islamic fundamentalist. They are totalitarian because they attempt to change and therefore control human nature. Dictatorships are terrible places for Jews and gays. They have to be. Whether or not Castro and Ahmadinejad are personally homophobes or anti-Semites, Iran and Cuba have to oppress Jews and gays. A regime that exists in order to propagate a political or religious belief suppresses all deviation. On the other hand, a state that accepts diversity is strengthened as diversity becomes accepted. It follows that just as democracy is good for Jews and gays, Jews and gays are good for democracy.

To Piers Lewis

Chapter 20

Reconsidering the Blessed Human Race

Cynicism is the theory that all human motivation is selfish. We lock our doors because we believe humanity is bad; we ask strangers for directions, which we follow, because we believe humanity is good. Even cynics are not afraid to request and accept directions.

Despite the fact that our society values kindness and admires selfless people, there is a current of popular cynicism that is reflected by such underground proverbs as "Never give a sucker an even break," or "No good deed goes unpunished," or even "The good die young." Half the collective ethos of our culture tells us to be good; the other half warns us that the good are exploited.

A belief in the natural badness of human beings has religious implications. If human nature is evil, human institutions cannot be any good either; humanity cannot save itself. Indeed, a poetic way to express cynicism is to say that man is born in original sin. Thus, cynicism is frequently linked with the idea of faith. Some religions teach that the reason to believe in God and to act morally is to achieve salvation. What is more cynical than being good solely because you want to be saved and not damned? Thus do faith and cynicism go hand in hand. A religion that looks upon morality as a question of reward and punishment not only reflects cynicism but teaches it as well.

Goodness, if practiced merely for the sake of reward, is not goodness at all but merely obedience. Reducing the very idea of morality to reward and punishment implies that ethical rules are arbitrary and incomprehensible in human terms.

Cynicism ignores and obscures the fact that the greatness of humanity lies in the heroism of the ordinary. In our everyday lives we rear our children and care for our parents, help out our neighbors and make major efforts for our friends, are courteous to strangers and careful about our surroundings. We do these things not because we expect to be rewarded but because we are good. When we don't act as we should, it is because we are too tired, too frightened, too pressed—because life is too hard.

The opposite of cynicism is politics, which reflects faith in human institutions. Politics is the legal acceptance of the necessity of both selfishness and altruism. In the long run they work together to insure human survival; in the short run they conflict with each other. That is why we need checks and balances. James Madison and the other authors of the Constitution were not being inconsistent when they gave power to the people and simultaneously guarded against the tyranny of the majority. Checks and balances, and the rule of law in general, recognize that the contradictions between individual and public needs are reconcilable. Indeed, this reconciliation is the purpose of law and government. That is why all societies have laws. Humans everywhere are political animals.

Philosophies that are based on the ultimate redemption of man in the next world—either in Heaven or after the Revolution—assume that the existing state of humanity is wicked and so have no choice but to deny the goodness of the ordinary. They also contain within themselves the mirror image of cynicism— the belief that those who have seen the light are capable of total goodness. This is quite logical; a belief in pure badness is the same as a belief in pure goodness—only with a minus sign in front of it. If human institutions have no value, neither do human goals. For cynics, therefore, goodness is identified with selflessness to the point of sacrifice.

Sacrifice and self-denial are considered virtues by Marxism and Christianity. In Christianity, suffering is redemptive; Jesus is the Lamb of God whose suffering takes away the sin of the world. The pain of ordinary mortals is redemptive as well; it is punishment here on earth for sins that will not have to be paid for again in the world to come. Marx, an atheist, could not very well speak about redemption, but Marxist societies extol sacrifice and confuse normal self-interest with bourgeois acquisitiveness.

Faith in human institutions, on the other hand, finds redemption in law—in accepting the goodness of human nature and the creativity of disagreement. Those who recognize that the tension between the individual and the group is normal can then work to redirect its energies in order to minimize conflict and injustice. A system of checks and balances is the legal realization of the recognition that the conflict between selfishness and altruism will never end. Marx and Jesus had no interest in checks and balances. Law was impotent in the evil world of today; it would become irrelevant and vanish in the perfect world of tomorrow.

If people are good, why is there so much violence and cruelty? One of the reasons is that human altruism is most frequently realized through nationalism, religion, and causes. One gets swept up in an issue which seems to embody the good; therefore, one does bad for the sake of doing good. The Khmer Rouge no doubt felt very virtuous. Pure altruism is even more dangerous than pure selfishness. Another reason for evil is fear, particularly fear of strangers and foreign customs. It is natural to dislike the ways of others—that is part of the instinct to adhere to the values of society. Foreignness looks very much like lawlessness to those who do not understand the vastness of the variety of human culture. The answer to xenophobia is politics—balancing the rights of those who fear the strange and those who are the strange.

We human beings have neither fangs, claws, nor armor. We cannot run very fast. To protect ourselves, we have formed small groups, like families, and larger groups, like clans, tribes and nations. We identify according to profession, age, sex, faith, politics, taste, etc. Our groups may be included within others, may intersect or may overlap. They are often in conflict with each other, just as individual needs are often in conflict with social needs. But these disagreements can be muted, controlled and redirected in a legal system that recognizes the inevitability of disagreement.

Prejudice is perhaps a logical consequence of division into groups: bonding among insiders has as its corollary suspicion of outsiders. The only societies that have not known racism are those that have not known about other races. Religious disagreements and national hostilities are so widespread that they seem to be inherent in the human experience. War has existed throughout history and in all parts of the world.

The establishment of the League of Nations and the United Nations is evidence that war has not always been considered inevitable. The League failed and the U.N. has not been especially successful, but the wars since 1945 have not been global, perhaps because of the existence of nuclear weapons. We still don't know whether the optimism reflected by the world's continued willingness to support the U.N. is justified. Nor do we know whether racism can be eliminated. The United States has outlawed segregated schools and has integrated public accommodations, but racial tensions remain. To the extent that a society seeks legal solutions to the problem of prejudice, it has rejected cynicism. Similarly, a world that attempts arms control and maintains peace-keeping forces in troubled areas is not an entirely cynical world. Politics may eventually be extended to control warfare among nations as it now does within nations.

Literature may be pro-cynicism or pro-politics. Lu Xun (1881-1936) is thought of as a political writer, yet his works are cynical in the extreme. He is highly respected in the People's Republic of China, where his dim view of humanity accords perfectly with Marxist ideology; his stories and essays are required reading in the schools. Lu Xun was no bleeding-heart liberal. In 1925 he wrote an essay called "'Fair Play' Should Be Put Off for the Time Being." Its Chinese title is *Tong da luo shui gou*, which means "severely beat a dog that has fallen into the water."

The Chinese title of this essay gives us a very good idea of its content: Have no pity on a dog or an enemy; strike him when he is down; fair play is an alien luxury. I don't know whether or not Lu's essay should be taken seriously. The essay shares with his stories an eerie quality that is reminiscent of Kafka. The voice of the essayist in "'Fair Play' Should Be Put Off for the Time Being" sounds to me like the voice of the crazy narrator in Lu's brilliant and imaginative "Diary of a Madman." Furthermore, Pierre Ryckmans, who writes under the pen-name Simon Leys, in a personal letter to me dated July 8, 1991, states, "Lu Xun's main mode of expression is irony (stating the reverse of his actual meaning), and he took Jonathan Swift as his model. Communist commentators are always lost when dealing with ironical essays—liberal readers should not experience such difficulties. Or do you believe that in his *Modest Proposal,* Swift was really advocating cannibalism?" Lu's countrymen, however, read him on only one level: simply a political writer whose essays and stories together form a unified attack against the feudal and Confucian values of pre-Liberation China.

If Lu is writing about how to behave in time of danger, his essay is superfluous. Revolutionaries and upholders of the old order are alike in their ruthlessness when they feel threatened. If he is giving us advice that is meant to be good for all time, he is not only nasty but mistaken. Hostility breeds more hostility.

In this savage essay by Lu Xun, harshness is being advocated in a totally rational style for purely practical ends. The writer suffers from lack of originality. If he were not trapped by tired old thoughts, he would know that goodness is not the same as weakness. His cynicism is nothing but laziness.

The Old Testament is very much about politics; it is the story of the establishment of human institutions in a particular time and place. The beginning of law is the development of the distinction between what is legal and what is illegal. This in turn presupposes the knowledge of what is good and evil. And yet in the Old Testament there is significant error about what is good and what is bad. We are told "Thou shalt not suffer a witch to live" (Exodus 22:18) despite the fact that there is no such thing as a witch. We are told "If a man lie with mankind, as he lieth with a woman, both of them have committed an abomination: they shall surely be put to death; their blood shall be upon them" (Leviticus 20:13) even though people with homosexual desires have always existed in all societies. If we think homosexuality is evil, that is because the Bible has told us so; there is no other reason. Fortunately, in a world where we talk, argue, and learn, we can continue to increase our understanding of morality.

Humanity separated itself from the rest of nature by discovering the idea of morality. This story is told figuratively in Genesis. Adam and Eve, like the birds and the bees, lived in innocence because they knew nothing else. They could no more be evil than a carnivorous animal or a deadly virus can be. By eating of the fruit of the Tree of Knowledge of Good and Evil, they entered a new stage of awareness that would inevitably lead to the building of social structures. They could take control of their fate rather than being the passive victims of the elements. In the words of the serpent, "and ye shall be as gods, knowing good from evil" (Gen. 3:5).

Adam and Eve paid the price inherent in civilization: alienated labor. "In the sweat of thy face shalt thou eat bread" (Gen. 3:19). Social organization also led to communal memory, longer than individual recollection. Therefore every human being learned that mortality was universal, that no individual could escape it, which was the fulfillment of God's warning to Adam about the forbidden fruit, "For in the day that thou eatest thereof, thou shalt surely die" (Gen. 2:17).

This beautiful story has been misinterpreted and trivialized. To say that humanity is wicked because of an act of disobedience by Adam and Eve is to deny the complexity of society and law, to lose sight of the fact that knowledge of evil is necessary in order to achieve justice, to forget that society—a prerequisite for both survival and civilization—is a human creation, to reject the view that law is a gift from heaven.

Mark Twain, in his essay, "The Damned Human Race," condemns Christianity and all religions for intolerance: "Man is the Religious Animal. . . . He is the only animal that has the True Religion—several of them. He is the only animal that loves his neighbor as himself, and cuts his throat if his theology isn't straight." Yet he accepts a traditional Christian reading of the doctrine of Original Sin: "What, now, do we find the primal Curse to have been? Plainly what it was in the beginning: the infliction upon man of the Moral Sense: the ability to distinguish good from evil; and with it, necessarily, the ability to *do* evil; for there can be no evil act without the presence of consciousness of it in the doer of it."

Mark Twain comes very close to understanding why the human race is blessed and not damned. What is missing from his analysis is law and politics, the recognition of the legitimacy of disagreement. Yes, the knowledge of evil creates evil in a world without law, rights and debate. This same knowledge defeats evil when combined with science, which is another word for acknowledging the possibility that one may be wrong.

Deng Xiaoping, in 1985, was admired and respected all over the world, just as Mikhail Gorbachev was in 1990. Deng and Gorbachev spoke about prosperity and practicality. They seemed to have lost faith in Marxist dogma. However, when the theocracies they ruled were threatened with real opposition, they showed themselves quite capable of human sacrifice. Unlike Abraham, Deng was not only able, but apparently even eager to sacrifice his children on June 4, 1989.

Totalitarianism was a 20th-century invention, but it is nevertheless a rejection of modernity. Totalitarian ideologies look back to an ideal time they claim existed in the past—a time of racial purity for the Nazis and of primitive communism for Marxists, a time when strife did not exist. The goal of such ideologies is the retention of contemporary technology but the rejection of all the other discordant features—questioning, variety, creativity—of modern life.

Although the Old Testament antedates both science and freedom, it recognizes the fact that time is linear. Events matter and change the course of history. History cannot be undone; the Garden of Eden is neither possible nor desirable; Adam and Eve's choices made us what we are.

Accepting the allegory of Adam and Eve cannot be confused with creationism. Chapter 1 of Genesis tells us that there is water above the sky. We have to read this as an allegory; there almost certainly was never a time in human history when people believed this. Furthermore, the Bible rejects the idea that the earth is round: "And God said, Let the waters under the heaven be gathered unto one place, and let the dry land appear: and it was so" (Gen. 1:9). We may, if we choose, argue that these words do not have to be interpreted as telling us that the world is flat; however, once we are willing to read the text in a more complex way, we could just as well say that the Bible does not reject evolution.

There is one Biblical passage where we cannot possibly find an interpretation that is scientifically acceptable. When Jacob knows that any newborn speckled sheep will belong to him, he places peeled rods before the parent sheep. "And the flocks conceived before the rods, and brought forth cattle ringstraked, speckled, and spotted" (Gen. 30:39). If this were presented as a miracle, we could believe it. Unfortunately, it is presented as science. Or maybe we should say "fortunately." The story of the speckled sheep is there to teach the world that we can't learn about science from Scripture.

The May 4th Movement, which was active in China in 1919, chose "Science and Democracy" as its slogan. A brilliant choice! Democracy and science are inseparable; both are reflections of modesty, of the fact that we need to look and listen and measure. Perhaps science and democracy are different aspects of a single phenomenon: searching. Both, through exploration and debate, reject cynicism and make politics possible. Science is the enemy of the grotesque superstition that had been persecuting China since Liberation. The Democracy Movement demanded science as well as freedom and democracy. The Movement understood these three things are inseparable. That is where its strength came from. Ironically, there is a May 4th Street in many Chinese cities, and May 4th is celebrated as a holiday, called "Students' Day."

What if people vote for repression? Voting is not the same thing as democracy, despite the etymology of the word. Voting is not enough; we need separation of powers and freedom of speech.

The scientific method—questioning, testing, measuring, drawing conclusions, and reconsidering them in the light of fresh evidence—is precisely what we mean by free speech. The Beijing Spring Movement of 1989 was a logical consequence of the May 4th Movement of 1919. Science and democracy are the gifts of the blessed human race. Democracy is the political realization of the scientific method.

INDEX